✺ THE ✺
CHORAL SINGER'S
SURVIVAL GUIDE

Courtesy of
Mike Murphy and Dwight Joyner,
GALA Choruses Board Member

GALA
CHORUSES

To my Mom and Dad,
Billy and Judy Thornton,
with a grateful heart for your
constant love and support

THE
CHORAL SINGER'S SURVIVAL GUIDE

Tony Thornton

VOCAL PLANET®

Vocal Planet Publishing, Inc.
Los Angeles, California

The Choral Singer's Survival Guide

Tony Thornton

Published by:
  Vocal Planet Publishing, Inc.
  Thomas LaFrance, CEO
  137 North Larchmont Boulevard, #494
  Los Angeles, CA 90004-3704
  info@vocalplanet.net
  www.vocalplanet.net

Manufactured in the United States of America

Library of Congress Cataloging-in-Publication Data

Thornton, Tony, 1967–
The choral singer's survival guide / Tony Thornton.
— 1st ed.
p. cm.
Includes bibliographical references and index.
  ISBN: 0-9762002-0-1 (paper)
    1. Choral singing—Instruction and study.
I. Thornton, Tony. II. Title. MT875.T46 2005 782.5'143
QBI04-200468

Design: Joseph Rattan Design
Editors: Marlene Head and Kate Peterson

CONTENTS

Foreword   ix
Preface   xi
Acknowledgments   xiii
About the Author   xv

1. THE CHORAL ARTIST   **1**
Why We Sing   2
"But I'm Tone Deaf ..."   2
The Benefits of Singing   3
How to Use This Book   3
Types of Ensembles   4
Finding the Right Choral Group for You   6
Gathering Audition Information and Requirements   7

2. PREPARING FOR A CHORAL AUDITION   **9**
Planning for the Audition   9
"Getting to Know You"   10
Preparation   11
Choosing a Solo Piece   12
Learning the Song   13

3. VOCAL TECHNIQUE   **17**
About the Voice   17
Sound Production   19
The Importance of Practice   19
How to Use the Companion CD   20
Body Alignment   20
Breath   24
Breathing Exercises   28
The Vocal Sound   31
The Vocal Cords   33
Vibrato   34
The Recipe for Beautiful Singing   34
Vocal Technique Exercises   35
Vocal Musicianship Exercises   43
CD Track Listing   50

4. THE AUDITION: BEFORE, DURING, AND AFTER   **51**
About Audition Anxiety   51
Getting Ready   52
Before the Audition   53
In the Audition Room   54
Performance Suggestions   54
Completing the Audition   55
The Waiting Game   55
The Audition Results   56
"Sorry, Better Luck Next Time"   57
"Congratulations! You're in the Chorus"   58

5. THE REHEARSAL   **61**
The First Rehearsal of the Season   62
Materials to Bring to Every Rehearsal   62
The Rehearsal Structure   63
Responsibilities of the Conductor   65
Responsibilities of the Singer   66
The Professional Singer   68
Rehearsal Tips   68
Additional Group Rehearsal Time   69
Private Rehearsal: Maximizing Your Efforts   70
Rehearsal Socials   71
The Dress Rehearsal   71

6. SCORE MARKING FOR SINGERS   **73**
General Markings   74
Tone and Text Markings   76
Intonation Markings   79
Tempo and Rhythm Markings   82
Phrase Markings   85

7. THE CHORAL PERFORMANCE   **89**
Become an Ambassador for Your Chorus   90
The Care and Preservation of the Voice   90
Concert Etiquette   92
Concert Preparation   94
"And the Crowd Goes Wild ..."   95
Afterglow   97

RESOURCES   **99**
Resource A: A Crash Course in Singers' Diction   101
   A Diction Primer   102
   English Diction   111
   Latin Diction (Roman Pronunciation)   116
   Italian Diction   122
   German Diction   128
   French Diction   134
Resource B: Musical Terms   145
Resource C: Key Signatures   151
Resource D: Vocal Ranges and Classifications   153
Resource E: Sight-Reading Tips and Suggestions   155
Resource F: Online Choral Music Resources   157
Resource G: Tips for a Successful Recording Session   163
Resource H: Travel Tips for Singers   165
Resource I: Summer Choral Festivals   169
Resource J: Professional Singing Opportunities   171
Resource K: From Singer to Conductor   173
Resource L: A Brief Overview of Choral Music History and Style   177

Glossary   187
Bibliography   213
Index   217

FOREWORD

The choral arts are flourishing, and participation in choruses of all types is booming. Every week, singers all over the country—in church choirs, community choruses, and professional choirs—are rehearsing and loving it. However, if you have never sung with a group before, where can you learn how to sing in a chorus? Where can you learn how to become a chorus member? And, once you are in the chorus, where can you learn the skills to become a fine or even a great chorister?

Look no further. Written by an expert singer and choral conductor, *The Choral Singer's Survival Guide* contains everything you need to take you from your first audition to the performance of a lifetime. This fine book is appropriate for experienced singers as well as for the person who has always thought about joining a chorus but did not know how to go about it. Practical and easy to read, the book provides clear and concise tips that you can immediately put to use.

If you are a beginning singer, you will quickly learn how to locate, prepare, and audition for a chorus that is a well-suited match. Singers of every level will find the expanded resource section an easy reference tool on topics such as proper diction in five languages, definitions of musical terms, and sight-reading tips. This is a book to which you will refer time and time again to review rehearsal techniques, score-marking, or work on your performance skills.

As you learn and apply the information in this book, your musicianship, confidence, performance quality, and overall musical experience will quickly grow. The accompanying CD contains breathing and vocal exercises, as well as vocal musicianship exercises, that you can integrate into your daily practice routine.

One section I found particularly helpful and supportive was the chapter on auditions. Auditioning can be a scary experience for many people—including *this* auditioner! The material here will help you prepare, which in turn will make the process easier and more comfortable. So go on—apply yourself, have courage, and know that you can do it. You will find enormous pleasure in singing in a group, well worth the time and effort.

The Choral Singer's Survival Guide should be in the library of every singer, choral conductor, and music teacher.

Vance George, Conductor
San Francisco Symphony Chorus

PREFACE

I am delighted and honored that you have chosen to read *The Choral Singer's Survival Guide*. My goal in writing it is to help you become the best choral musician you can be and to provide accessible information that will help you achieve that goal.

Since before I can remember, my life has been filled with vocal music. As a baby, my mother would sing to me often, and my relatives tell me that I began singing before I spoke my first word. As a very shy and introverted child, I found it difficult to make new friends, as I did not really do well in social settings. I was scrawny and had a very high and soft voice for a boy, so I was a very self-conscious kid all around. Through singing and the study of music—specifically, singing as part of the chorus in junior high school and high school—I was able to build relationships with other students, learn discipline, and grow in self-confidence. Although I enjoyed my other subjects, chorus was the reason I got up each morning to go to school.

Studies have shown that, in many cases, early exposure to the arts is what prompts us to continue serving the arts for a lifetime. So my own early exposure to music is perhaps what has compelled me to dedicate my life to the service of music and, in particular, choral music.

For most of my life, I was on the other side of the baton. During my college years, I had the privilege of singing under the baton of some of the most gifted conductors in the world, and for several years, I performed as a member of the Robert Shaw Festival Singers. Now, as a conductor, I audition and work with singers on a regular basis.

Although there are a great many books written for conductors, there are very few materials written specifically for choral singers. I have found that many singers do not have access to the information that will help them match the right chorus with their skills and needs, teach them how to properly prepare for auditions, provide a uniform approach to score marking, and give them the tools to develop their rehearsal and performance skills. Considering that there are nearly 30 million choral singers in the United States alone—not to mention the millions of other choral singers across the globe—there is a great need for choral singers to have a concise companion guide to the many facets of choral singing.

The Choral Singer's Survival Guide is for choral singers of all ages as well as established singers who make part of their living by singing in a chorus. In it, you will find valuable information that will help you become a great choral musician, one whom everyone envies. If you are not currently singing in a choral ensemble, *The Choral Singer's Survival Guide* will help you prepare for a successful audition and set you on the road to a wonderful musical experience. In addition, I hope my fellow conductors, both experienced and up-and-coming, will find this guide a valuable resource they can refer to and share with their chorus members.

Singing is a learned skill that requires practice. The companion CD offers many invaluable exercises and tips to prepare you vocally for an audition and to use on a daily basis to keep improving the sound and quality of your voice.

In the resource section, you will find information on such subjects as diction, musical terms, sight-reading, and online choral resources, including a list of interactive websites that instruct choral singers on the basics of music theory and music reading. Several websites are also referenced in the text portion of the book.

As you apply and practice your new musical knowledge and skills, you will find that weekly rehearsals and performances move to a higher level than you ever thought possible. More important, as you grow musically, you will inspire those around you to grow as well, thus raising the level of artistry in your own chorus and, in the larger scheme of things, the quality of choral music worldwide.

Thank you for investing your talent, time, and passion in the choral arts. Keep singing!

Tony Thornton
Los Angeles, California

ACKNOWLEDGMENTS

We do not create alone. As artists, we constantly receive inspiration and insight from those around us. It is with love and gratitude that I offer thanks to the following people:

To my sister, Leslie Cromer, for always being there for me. I love you very much. To Scot Cromer, my brother-in-law, it's great to have you in our family.

To Doris Preston and Helen Thornton, my beloved grandmothers, and in loving memory of my grandfathers, F. R. Preston and Jess W. ("Tiny") Thornton. Thank you for always inspiring me to reach higher and higher and for keeping me grounded when I stray.

To my aunts, uncles, and cousins who have helped shape me into the person I am today: Michael and Patsy Patterson, Maureen Peterson, David and Marcia Preston, Gary and Shellia Preston, Thomas Preston and in loving memory of Nancy Preston, Geraldine Redden, Bruce, Calva, Diane, Jeff, Jennifer, Kelly, Kevin, Robby, Ryan, Scott, and Selena.

To Thomas LaFrance, CEO of Vocal Planet Publishing, for believing in this project and for giving a voice to my work through publishing this book. You are truly amazing and a wonderful friend.

To my best friends, Bill Usher, Stephen Powers, and Pär Sjöblom. Thank you for always challenging me and making me laugh. You guys are the best.

To my friend, Bryce Fujii. Thank you for encouraging me to complete this book and for your belief in me and my work.

To the singers and board of directors of Los Angeles Choral Artists. It is a pleasure to work with such a fantastic organization. Here's to many more years of wonderful music making.

To my colleagues, mentors, and teachers: Patty Breitag, Samuel Brown, Lindsey Christiansen, Joseph Flummerfelt, Kenneth Fulton, the late Frauke Haasemann, James Jordan, Iris Levine, Bruce Mayhall, James Mulholland, Judith Nicosia, Donald Neuen, Janet Noll, the late Robert Shaw, and Constantina Tsolainou. Thank you for challenging me to reach deep inside myself to discover the music within.

I have learned much of the knowledge contained in this book from the many students I have taught in educational institutions, privately, in workshops, or in the nonprofit arena. Thanks to all of my students, past and present, for giving me so much. I especially want to thank West Coast Singers for seven years of music making.

To my editors, Marlene Head and Kate Peterson. I am so grateful for your extraordinary work on this book.

Thanks to my friends at Media Creature Music, especially Sharal Churchill, for the recording of the companion CD to this book. Additional thanks to Nathanael Lew, John Hiler, and Kathryn Korniloff for editing the CD.

To Jon Bailey for your considerable voice-over talent in narration and to Diana Jaramillo, whose lovely voice graces the tracks of the companion CD.

To the marvelous Vance George. Your contributions to choral music are enormous. To say that I am honored to have you write the foreword to my book would be an understatement. Thank you for your friendship and support.

To Katy Bowen and David Long for providing the illustrations and music examples for the book. Thank you for helping to bring the visual representation of my words to life.

To Joe Rattan and Glenn Hadsall. Without a designer and typesetter, a book just looks like a longer-than-usual term paper. Thank you for your creative vision in designing the cover and setting the text. You are wonderful.

To Jason Thatcher. Thanks for serving as the model for alignment in the vocal techniques chapter.

To my reviewers, Duke Anderson, Kenneth Fulton, William Hanrahan, Robyn Frey-Monell, Joel Peisinger, Lynn Thompson, and Constantina Tsolainou. Thank you for taking time out of your busy schedules. Your expert advice helped to shape this book into a stronger tool for singers.

To my high school choral director, Tom Cole. Your guidance and belief in my abilities as a young singer and pianist was a major influence in my life. For that, I am eternally grateful.

ABOUT THE AUTHOR

Photo: James Berglund

A native of Alabama, Tony Thornton received his Bachelor of Music degree in Music Education and Voice from Westminster Choir College and a Master of Music degree in Choral Conducting from Louisiana State University. While a student at Westminster Choir College, he was a John Finley Williamson Scholar for four years. As a member of the Westminster Choir, he performed at the Spoleto Festivals in both Italy and the United States, and he has recorded with Leonard Bernstein, Riccardo Muti, Claudio Abbado, and Zubin Mehta.

Graduating with highest honors from Louisiana State University in 1992, Thornton conducted the LSU Men's Chorus and was assistant director of the A Cappella Choir, Chamber Singers, and University Chorus. He has studied conducting with Joseph Flummerfelt, Frauke Haasemann, Margaret Hillis, Kenneth Fulton, Constantina Tsolainou, and Donald Neuen. He sang for eight years as a member of the Grammy Award–winning Robert Shaw Festival Singers, and he has performed as a guest soloist throughout the United States, Asia, and Europe. In addition, he has been a guest lecturer of music at UCLA, Pomona College, Los Angeles City College, and CSU–Pomona.

For seven years, Thornton served as the Artistic Director of West Coast Singers. He is currently the Founding Artistic Director of Los Angeles Choral Artists, which made its debut in 2003. He teaches voice in workshops as well as privately in Los Angeles, and he frequently is invited to conduct workshops with choruses throughout the country.

THE CHORAL ARTIST

"To be an artist is not the privilege of a few,
but the necessity of us all."

Robert Shaw

e are all artists. Some artists paint pictures. Others become actors, writers, dancers, or composers. And millions of us choose to express our artistry through singing. In fact, a recent survey compiled by Chorus America (www.chorusamerica.org) estimates that nearly 30 million Americans regularly perform in choral ensembles, making choral singing America's number-one art form—and this estimate does not include the millions of choral singers in other countries around the world.

Despite severe cuts in arts funding during the late 1990s and early 2000s, choral music—music written for more than one singer on a part—is still thriving. The fact that the choral medium has continued to grow during this time attests to its significance in providing pleasure and enrichment to our lives.

WHY WE SING

The human voice Is our original instrument. There is not a culture on the planet that does not have singers. Because you have chosen to read this book, most likely you are either a choral singer already or someone who is interested in joining a chorus.

Singers join choruses for a variety of reasons. Some find a creative or social outlet in singing together. Many people sing in a chorus to enrich their own lives and to touch the hearts and souls of their audiences. Still others sing for the intellectual stimulation that comes from learning the choral masterworks.

One of the most wonderful rewards of choral ensemble singing is the opportunity to create something more beautiful than any one singer could create alone. When you contribute your talents as a choral singer to the artistic life of your community and the world, you help enrich our collective culture and nurture the spirit of our planet.

Music also provides much-needed balance in our lives. When misfortune strikes, a natural tendency during the grieving process is for us to come together and sing as way to begin healing. I personally believe there is no more universal language than music and that it is often only through music that we can express the otherwise inexpressible—and change the hearts and minds of people for the better.

"BUT I'M TONE DEAF"

Tone deafness is the inability to distinguish differences in pitch or reproduce them. Considering that only 2% of the population is clinically tone deaf, there is a very good chance that you do not fit into this category. Perhaps you believe you can't sing because you were told to "mouth the words and let the others carry the tune" as a young child. Not only is this psychologically distressing and embarrassing to a young singer, it may result in a lifelong—as well as sad and unnecessary—self-exile from music.

The good news is that a majority of these uninformed pronouncements are incorrect. With a little work, it is possible to improve one's listening skills and learn how to discern changes in pitch. If a nonmedical person has told your child that he or she is tone deaf, consult a health professional immediately to verify—or disprove—the "diagnosis."

Take Note

There are approximately 250,000 choruses in the United States: 12,000 professional and community choruses, at least 38,000 school choruses, and 200,000 church choirs. There are probably more choruses than any other kind of performing arts organizations in the country.

Chorus America
America's Performing Art: A Study of Choruses, Choral Singers and Their Impact, p. 3

THE BENEFITS OF SINGING

Singing benefits us in ways we do not completely understand. Many writers have described the positive physical, mental, emotional, and spiritual effects of music. Some even believe music will be the medicine of the future.

Singing in a chorus improves creativity, social skills, community involvement, academic skills, listening skills, team-building skills, discipline, and political awareness. In addition, singing with others helps bridge social gaps, allowing us to connect with people of different social, ethnic, and religious backgrounds. A wealth of multicultural choral music provides singers the opportunity to experience the music and language of others.

HOW TO USE THIS BOOK

The Choral Singer's Survival Guide is designed to guide singers through the choral process, from searching and auditioning for the right chorus all the way to the final performance. Helpful suggestions are included for increasing both your likelihood of success at the audition and your performance quality once accepted into a chorus. Tips are included throughout the book. For parents of young singers, the tips in "A Note to Parents" provide helpful information.

The resource section contains reference materials and online resources for further study. Useful information about diction, choral history and style, musical terms, professional singing opportunities, and travel tips is available at your fingertips.

The companion CD guides you through vocal exercises to increase resonance, range, power, and tone quality. Vocal Musicianship Exercises are included to teach you how to execute many of the most common musical elements of the score, including how to improve intonation, properly crescendo/decrescendo, and sing an accent or staccato.

It is an honor to be your guide. Whether you are a choral singer in a church choir, professional choir, symphony chorus, or school chorus, or a singer looking to join a chorus, the information contained in this book will help you focus your goals and refine your skills.

TYPES OF ENSEMBLES

Choral programs come in all shapes and sizes. Below are some of the most common types of choral ensembles.

Educational Organizations

Fine programs still exist despite unfortunate cuts to many music programs in elementary, middle, and high schools across the country.

At the elementary school level, students may have music only once or twice per week for half an hour. If there is a full-time music teacher, a children's choir program composed of both boys and girls may be developed as part of the music curriculum.

As the student enters middle or junior high school, opportunities usually exist to perform in either a boys' or a girls' choir, or as a member of a mixed chorus.

At the high school level, the choral student may continue to perform in a boys', girls', or mixed chorus. Additional groups may include jazz or pop choirs, a madrigal choir, or a chamber choir for the more advanced students.

Colleges around the country provide music majors and nonmajors the opportunity to perform in a variety of choral ensembles. Men's, women's, and mixed choruses, including oratorio choirs, early music ensembles, madrigal choirs, chamber choirs, and opera and musical theatre choruses, may be available to the student. In some cases, a symphonic chorus, such as the one at Westminster Choir College of Rider University (www.rider.edu/Westminster/), exposes singers to major choral works with orchestra, under the baton of world-renowned conductors and orchestras.

Nonprofit Choral Organizations

Volunteer Community Choruses

As educational institutions at the elementary, middle, and high school levels continue to cut music programs from the curriculum, the community chorus has emerged as a leader in the choral arts.

Men's, women's, and mixed choruses, encompassing a wide range of styles, exist to present concerts to the general public. Barbershop men's and women's groups, gospel choirs, children's and youth choirs, early music groups, and opera and musical theatre choruses represent just a few of the ensembles available to singers. Some businesses or corporations have their own choirs made up of company employees. Groups such as this may perform at special events or during the holidays to market the company.

It is possible for volunteer singers to reach professional standards in performance. The Atlanta Symphony Chorus (www.asochorus.org), founded by the late Robert Shaw, is composed entirely of volunteer singers, yet the chorus has received 12 Grammy awards for its critically acclaimed recordings.

Church Choirs

There are more church choirs in the country than any other type of choral organization. The sheer number of church choirs (about 200,000, according to Chorus America) is the most likely reason that so many of us received our first training as a chorister in church.

Groups Containing Both Volunteer and Professional Singers

Although some church choirs are composed entirely of volunteer singers, others employ professional singers to advance the group. Paid singers ideally provide a model sound and professional skills that the volunteer singers will emulate, thus raising the level of performance.

Community choruses, especially mixed choruses, often follow the church model. Symphony, opera, and musical theatre groups around the country make use of a volunteer/professional mix to great success.

Fully Professional Ensembles

Some choruses, such as symphony, chamber, opera, and musical theatre groups, have the financial resources available to pay every singer in the ensemble. However, a singer pursuing a professional career in music today must often supplement his or her income with either a full-time job or other singing engagements.

Chanticleer (www.chanticleer.org), the renowned men's ensemble, pays each singer a full-time salary, as the group normally tours an average of 25 weeks each year.

A Note to Parents

I am the only musician in my family. Although classical music was not played in my home while I was growing up, I was encouraged to sing at a very young age. Early exposure to music sets the stage for a lifelong interest in music.

Sing to your child, and encourage your child to sing with you. You do not need to have the best voice in the world. A child will usually become involved in choral music if one or both parents sing in a choral ensemble or at least make music an active part of home life.

Let principals, the school board, community leaders, other parents, and teachers know that you consider the arts an integral part of your child's education. We often assume that everyone values the importance of the arts. Some, however, may consider the arts a luxury rather than a necessary part of our growth and development.

FINDING THE RIGHT CHORAL GROUP FOR YOU

The Internet is a wonderful place to begin when researching choruses in your area. Google™ (www.google.com) and Yahoo!® (www.yahoo.com) are good search engines, and many choruses have websites that include audition requirements and dates along with concert and organizational information.

ChoralNet (www.choralnet.org) lists thousands of choir websites on its site. In addition, the ChoralNet Auditions Forum contains information about ongoing auditions as well as a "Choirs Wanted" area for singers who are searching for a choir.

The ChoralNet Job Board lists openings for paid chorus members, section leaders, and soloists.

Some choruses post their audition announcements on community bulletin boards, in newspapers, or in trade papers. Choruses sometimes announce auditions in their concert programs. Major newspapers and weekly papers usually include a music section or calendar section that contains concert performance information. The Chorus America website (www.chorusamerica.org) contains a concert calendar of performances by its member choruses.

GATHERING AUDITION INFORMATION AND REQUIREMENTS

Choruses hold auditions at various times during the year. High school and middle school choruses often audition at the end of the previous year. College choral auditions may occur at the end of the previous year or before the beginning of the term. Most community choruses audition prior to the first rehearsal of the season. Some choruses hold open auditions, where potential members come to one or two rehearsals prior to the audition. This allows a singer to get a feel for the group and the conductor before scheduling an audition. Some choruses even hold midyear auditions for new members.

Every situation is different, and the requirements vary depending on the nature of the ensemble. In the research phase, long before you schedule an audition for a particular group, try to get to know as much about it as possible.

Use the list of suggestions and questions below to help you decide if an ensemble is right for you. You can find many of the items on this list on chorus websites.

▸ What is the chorus's mission statement? Make sure you can support it before continuing your research. Some conductors provide a vision statement for the group as well.
▸ What is the professional and educational background of the conductor and key staff?
▸ What is the size of the chorus (e.g., a small chamber group or a large symphonic chorus)?
▸ What type of literature does the chorus perform?
▸ Does your voice suit this group's style of music and performance?
▸ When do auditions take place?
▸ Is it possible to sit in on a rehearsal prior to the audition?

▸ What is the time commitment to the chorus? Make sure you can fully commit to the schedule *before* you audition.
▸ What is the financial commitment? Some choruses require dues from their members. (However, dues are usually less per month than a movie and dinner. The opportunity to sing is well worth the investment in your life.)
▸ Is there a sight-reading requirement? If so, what level of sight-reading is necessary?
▸ Is a prepared solo required for the audition? If so, what type of piece is appropriate?
▸ Will there be a musical skills test?
▸ Will there be an interview? If so, who will do the interviewing?
▸ Are there callbacks?
▸ Are chorus members expected to serve on a committee or do other volunteer tasks beyond singing?

Be sure you have completed your research before setting up an audition. In addition, once you have located two or three choruses you are interested in, attend a concert of theirs prior to setting up an audition. This can quickly give you enough information to decide whether a chorus is a match for your needs.

Do not simply audition for the first group you come across. Audition for a group you are passionate about musically. Make sure your skill level matches the requirements of the group. You will want to stretch a bit musically, but not quite so far that you get in over your head.

Now that you have gathered all the appropriate information, it is time to begin preparing for the audition.

CHAPTER

PREPARING FOR A CHORAL AUDITION

onductors audition singers in a variety of ways, depending on the skills needed for the ensemble. A professional chorus audition may require a singer to sing individually, whereas another ensemble may audition singers in a small group. There are many audition situations, and you will want to make sure that you are prepared with the right questions and answers whatever the requirement.

PLANNING FOR THE AUDITION

Many singers do not plan for a successful audition. Lack of planning and preparation may heighten feelings of fear. However, proper planning and knowledge will set the stage for a more successful experience as well as help relieve some of the fear associated with auditioning. The more you know about the group and the conductor, the better.

In the best-case scenario, a potential singer will be familiar with the ensemble through having attended a concert prior to the audition. This is very important for a couple of reasons. One, it gives the singer a more realistic picture of the organization. Two, it fuels excitement about the organization—and the potential singer, if selected, will most likely continue in the group for many years.

On the flip side, singers who audition without carefully researching may often end up leaving because the ensemble was not what they expected. When this happens, not only is the chorus hurt by having an unforeseen section gap, it also means much time will have been wasted on the part of the conductor and the singer. However, the guidelines in this book will help to prevent this from happening to you (or the ensemble).

The rest of this chapter will give you the tools you need to (1) ensure that the ensemble you are auditioning for is a match for your goals as a singer and (2) make the most of your audition.

"GETTING TO KNOW YOU"

To begin with, you will want to learn all you can about the group. There are several ways to accomplish this and, if possible, you should do all of the following:

1. Attend one or two concerts before the audition.
2. Ask to sit in on a couple of rehearsals. Get to know the conductor's work ethic and the areas emphasized musically in rehearsal. Make sure you are a master of these things at your audition. You may also want to find out the pieces the group will be rehearsing during your visit and practice the music at home as if you are already a member of the ensemble. This initial effort will show commitment on your part, which is paramount for a successful choral ensemble.
3. Speak with current chorus members to learn about their experiences with the ensemble and the conductor.

If you now feel the group is a good match, contact the chorus to schedule an audition.

PREPARATION

The amount of prep time a singer needs for an audition depends on his or her stage of musical development. Singers who audition on a regular basis (especially professional singers) are able to audition successfully within days of learning about an audition. Other singers may need weeks, months, or perhaps an entire season to prepare musically for the audition. The key to your success is to learn the exact requirements of the audition. This information will help you weigh your current musical skills against the audition requirements. An honest evaluation will help you prepare more completely, increasing the likelihood both that the audition experience will represent your true skills and that the choral organization will accept you. Follow these guidelines to prepare for your audition.

▸ Practice the vocal exercises in Chapter 3 daily. If you need more intense work, study privately prior to auditioning for a choral ensemble. Your voice teacher will work with you on scales, sight-reading, and tonal memory exercises. Remember, the first thing the conductor will want to hear is a beautiful tone. Study with a member of the National Association of Teachers of Singing (NATS). Its website (www.nats.org) may have a list of teachers in your area. Another great resource is www.voiceteachers.com. Listings on the website are by state, and the site is easy to use.

▸ Depending on the requirements of the audition, you may want to enroll in a sight-reading or music theory course at your local college or community college. A private tutor is even better. Accessing the knowledge of an advanced music student at a local college or university is great experience for the student—and it will save you money.

▸ If hiring a voice teacher or theory tutor is not an option financially, practice with a friend who plays piano—and if the friend has a vocal or choral background, even better. Set up a mock audition involving all elements required for the audition. If the audition includes an interview, include interview questions. "Why would you like to join the ensemble?" and "What skills, musical or otherwise, would you bring to the group?" are questions that should be considered in any case.

▸ Practice sight-reading hymns (or Bach chorales for more of a challenge) to sharpen your music reading skills. (Review the sight-reading tips in Resource E. Also, see "Music Theory, Sight-Reading, and Music History" in Resource F: Online Choral Music Resources.)

▶ If required, choose the solo piece (see the next section for tips on how to do this). Your voice teacher, if you have one, is a great resource for song selection and preparation. Some conductors may ask you to sing a hymn or a specific piece such as *The Star Spangled Banner* or *My Country 'Tis of Thee*.

▶ Visualize a successful audition. In your mind's eye, see the room, the conductor, and the accompanist. Visualize yourself relaxed, yet confident. You are focused and performing at the top of your ability. Many of the world's most successful people use visualization techniques on a regular basis.

CHOOSING A SOLO PIECE

The choice of the solo is critical to the success of your audition. If you must choose your own song without the help of a voice teacher, consider the following points when selecting the piece for the audition:

▶ Do not choose a song simply because you like it. Liking the piece is important, but the song you choose should flatter your voice and show off your musical skills while staying within the guidelines of the audition. For example, you may be required to sing a song from an opera or oratorio. Give them what they ask for.

▶ Choose a song that you know well and that is within your vocal range and skills as a musician. Remember, when you sing this song, you will likely feel nervous. Make sure you select a piece that allows you to shine vocally during the audition.

▶ Do not choose a song with an extremely difficult accompaniment, as the pianist may be sight-reading the piece. Make sure the music is written in the correct key. If the music is not available in the correct key, either select another piece or have someone transpose it for you. If the music is transposed, professionally notate it using a program such as Finale® or Sibelius. Do not expect the accompanist to transpose for you on the spot unless you have cleared this with a staff member or the conductor prior to the audition. If there are other changes, mark them in the score, as you may or may not have time to rehearse with the accompanist prior to auditioning.

▶ If possible, prepare a second song in a contrasting style in the event you are asked to demonstrate your musical versatility. In addition, having more than one song memorized and ready to sing gives you options for other auditions.

LEARNING THE SONG

After you have chosen the song, the next step is to learn it thoroughly. The learning process for a solo song is similar to the learning process of a choral piece. However, for a choral piece you would receive much of the information below either during your rehearsal or from performance notes at the choral rehearsal.

You will need to call upon your practice partner once again. Begin by recording only the melody of the song. After recording the melody only, record a second version with the piano accompaniment only. To better understand the piece, look up the dates of the composer and identify the period and style of the song.

As in a choral rehearsal, the first step in learning a new piece is to mark breaths in the music score (see Chapter 6). Breath management is a major part of a singer's development. Placing breath marks in the musical score will help you learn to pace your breath and spin out the vocal line. This is so simple, and yet singers often begin the learning process without this crucial step. If you do not write breath marks into the score, you will tend to breathe anywhere, creating inconsistency in the vocal line.

As you work through the piece, determine its overall structure. Do sections of the song repeat? If so, is it an exact repetition?

Now, go to the CD (see Chapter 3) and warm up your voice before you continue. Follow the warm-up process carefully, working on alignment, breath, and then sound. Get in the habit of warming up prior to any sort of vocal rehearsal or speaking engagement.

A good way to determine where breath marks should appear in the music is to separate the text from the music. Type or write out the text. Read the text aloud and identify potential breaths, important words, and phrase lengths. Your muscles begin to memorize body posture immediately, so when reading aloud, remember to maintain correct body alignment (see Chapter 3). Pronounce the words as you would sing them, with very tall vowel sounds and crisp consonants. Read the text as if you are a great orator. This initial effort will carry over into singing later on, saving you time in the overall learning process.

While reading the text aloud, begin to determine the meaning and mood of the song. What is the song about? Is it happy or sad? Look up words you do not understand in the dictionary. One word can change the entire meaning and interpretation of a song. If you are unsure about anything, look it up. Writing a one-sentence description or choosing a keyword for the piece can be very helpful. The description or keyword will help you stay focused on the meaning and mood of the piece.

If the song is in a foreign language, learn the correct pronunciation (see Resource A: A Crash Course in Singers' Diction) and find an exact, word-by-word translation of the song. The translation included under the text in your score may be inaccurate or inadequate. A voice teacher or a language expert at a local college or university can be of great assistance. In larger libraries, singers may use resources such as *Word-by-Word Translations of Songs and Arias* by Berton Coffin, Werner Singer, and Pierre Delattre or *The Interpretation of French Song* by Pierre Bernac for correct translations of the text. If these options are not available, and you are not proficient in foreign languages, choose a piece in your native tongue.

Now that you have identified breaths, important words, and phrases, transfer your markings into the music score. Circle or highlight dynamics and draw in any crescendos that are not already in the score (see Chapter 6). This may seem like more effort than necessary, but be assured that this careful preparation will make the learning process easier in the long run and increase your musicality immensely. What we are doing here is building the song layer by layer. Since we learn in layers, it makes sense to approach the song-learning process in this way.

Before adding notes, identify difficult rhythm patterns and work these out first. As Robert Shaw often said in rehearsal, "The right note at the wrong time is the wrong note." Master the rhythm first and the pitches will more easily fall into place (at the right time).

Next, speak the text in rhythm while listening to the melody-only version you recorded. Stay true to your breath marks and the musical phrase. Speak with wonderful tone at about a *mezzo piano* level without changes in dynamic or crescendos/decrescendos. We only want to solidify the rhythm and text at this point. The other layers will come next. You may need to read the text along with the recording several times to become secure with the rhythm of the text:

Once you are completely secure with the text, rhythm, and meaning of the song, begin to add the proper notes by singing along with the recorded melody-only version. Focus on beautiful tone as you add the notes. If possible, practice near a mirror so that you can monitor that you are singing with tall vowels and that you are communicating the song facially.

Be sure to study the accompaniment. Does the accompaniment double your part? When you are completely secure with the notes, practice with the accompanied version. Add dynamics and everything else called for on the page. Use the Vocal Musicianship Exercises in Chapter 3 and the companion CD to reinforce your mastery of the interpretive elements of the musical score. As an artist, your goal is to bring to life musically everything seen (and unseen) on the page.

Memorize the song. Song memory includes more than just the text and the notes; all of the interpretive elements included in the score must be memorized. If you have completed each step above in sequence, you will probably find that you have the song mostly memorized. However, if you need further help memorizing, try the following tips:

▸ Repeat the text away from the music to help you fully memorize the words. Write the words on paper and read the text aloud as a poem.
▸ After you have memorized the text, add the notes phrase-by-phrase. When you can sing the first phrase perfectly at least three times with correct notes and musicianship, begin work on the next phrase. Add the phrases together as you memorize them so that you sing two phrases perfectly, then three, and so on.
▸ Do not use the score as a crutch. You probably know more than you think you know.
▸ Do not try to cram.
▸ Choose a keyword for each phrase to help you remember the character and meaning.
▸ Try working backward. Start at the end of the piece and work toward the beginning.
▸ Visualize the music. Drawing pictures to represent your concept of the mood and interpretation will aid your memory.
▸ After you have memorized the music, sing the song in your head while working around the house or at breaks during the workday.
▸ Study the music just before you go to bed. Studying right before sleep will increase your ability to remember the finer details in the musical score.
▸ If a section of the work repeats elsewhere, do not try to rememorize it. Many singers tend to learn music from cover to cover, only to realize later that one section is the same or very similar to a section already learned.
▸ Sing the song to another person and explain your interpretation of the song to him or her.
▸ Perform the song with live piano accompaniment for a small audience and invite feedback. Get the family involved and, if possible, invite a couple of experienced singers to hear you. This will be great practice, and you will receive helpful advice in a supportive atmosphere.

Congratulations! You have laid the groundwork for a successful audition experience. Now, let's work on your vocal technique.

CHAPTER

VOCAL TECHNIQUE

ow that you have researched the chorus you are interested in joining, it is time to get your voice in shape for the audition. A great sound alone generally will not get you into an ensemble, but it *is* a major factor in the decision-making process.

ABOUT THE VOICE

The human voice is a truly unique instrument, and it is both a thrill and a gift to be able to sing and join with other voices in song. The voice sits halfway between the brain and the heart, and it takes both to become a great singer.

Unlike other instruments, the voice—a wind instrument—is the only instrument that can produce words; is capable of developing good or bad habits; is connected to the brain, whose structure, made of muscle, bone, and cartilage, is mostly hidden inside the body; cannot be "played" in times of sickness; and can take in food and water and make a sound through the same space. Most of us may not be able to afford a Steinway to make music with, but the voice is part of all of us—and it's free!

Our voices, according to most accepted theories, are composed of three registers: chest, middle, and head voice. The most beautiful voices flow from top to bottom—and back—without any noticeable lifts, or breaks. Using the term *lift* is more useful in showing how to remedy the problem. Although these lifts in the scale are inconsistent in the immature or untrained voice, high voices tend to have a universal register change on the note F, medium voices on E, and lower voices on D (see figure 3.1).

Figure 3.1 Changes in Register

To overcome a very noticeable change in register, lighten the tone quality and sing with a feeling of lift as you approach an area of transition in the voice. Be sure to also pace the breath (see Breath Exercise 2 on the CD). The exercises at the end of this chapter will help you begin to move smoothly from one register to the next more efficiently.

SOUND PRODUCTION

To produce any sound successfully, an initiator, a vibrator, a resonator, and a receiver are needed. The *initiator* of the voice is the brain, which gives the impulse for breath (the motor of the voice); the *vibrator* is the vocal folds; the *resonator* is the entire body, especially the cavities above the larynx, including the mouth; and the *receiver* is the ears of the singer and eventually those of the audience.

Musical and vocal skills are built by coordinating the elements above through practice. Practice is necessary to reinforce correct alignment, breath, and sound. Begin every practice session with body alignment and breathing exercises. The term *alignment* is preferred rather than *posture*, as many singers tend to hold, rather than balance, the body when they are told by a conductor or voice teacher that they need to have better posture. This creates tension in the body. To produce a wonderful sound, body alignment and breath must be prepared prior to singing. Only when alignment is correct can air enter the body easily, aiding in the production of a free and uninhibited vocal sound.

THE IMPORTANCE OF PRACTICE

Athletes practice five to six days per week, and so should singers. As a singer, you are developing your "vocal muscle," which needs consistent exercise so that the muscles of the body involved in singing can perform the same functions over and over again. The more you practice, the faster you will progress vocally.

Although the need for practice seems quite obvious, many singers do not prepare adequately for rehearsals or performances. Setting up a consistent practice schedule now can (1) establish the routine necessary for when you are accepted into the chorus and (2) get you on track for a better musical experience.

To consistently improve your vocal and musical skills, at least 30 minutes of practice per day is recommended for adults and 20 minutes per day for children and youths. Practice does not have to take place in one session. Adults can break up their practice time into two sessions of 15 minutes each, and children and youths can practice for 10 minutes twice a day. A warm-up in the morning before the day begins and another midday session to reinforce alignment, deep-seated breathing, and a healthy speaking voice will help protect you from vocal damage and fatigue. If your job requires you to do a lot of speaking, the exercises reinforcing correct alignment and breath also will help you speak more clearly, so that you leave work energized rather than vocally exhausted.

Use these exercises daily to continue building your sound. As a practice routine, always start with proper alignment, work with one or two of the breath exercises (always including Breath Exercise 2), and then move to the vocal exercises.

HOW TO USE THE COMPANION CD

The companion CD will bring to life many of the exercises in the book. A symbol

appears next to each exercise contained on the CD. Read through the exercise once or twice, then simply follow the instructions on the CD. As you are performing each exercise, you will be given important tips. Note that all consonants and vowels in the exercises use International Phonetic Alphabet (IPA) symbols. See the Diction Primer in Resource A: A Crash Course in Singers' Diction for questions regarding IPA.

As you become familiar with the exercises, select from the list each day for your daily warm-up. Once the exercises are established in your ear, perform them without the accompaniment. Take your pitch from a piano, pitch pipe, or tuning fork. Working in this manner will strengthen your aural skills and your voice.

BODY ALIGNMENT

Correct alignment is essential to produce your best possible tone. If there is tightening or pressure in any area of the body, the breath cannot enter the body efficiently. This in turn causes a "short circuit" in the body's internal information system resulting in a constricted vocal sound. In addition, your muscles tend to "memorize" the position of your body as you sing. Therefore, if your body is learning incorrect alignment while you practice a song, it will most likely "remember" and reproduce that position during your audition, rehearsal, and performance—even when you sing that song again years down the road.

Proper alignment during your private practice time and in the choral rehearsal will help solve many intonation, sound, and rhythm problems in your music study. It will also carry over into daily life with positive effects. As singers, we want to sing with our entire being, and proper alignment is the first step on the way toward creating a powerful, engaging sound (see figure 3.2).

 Correct Body Alignment (Standing) From Toe to Head (Track 3)

▸ Your feet should be shoulder-width apart, with one foot just a bit in front of the other. This foot position helps create a more energetic stance when performing and prevents locked knees, which can cause fainting.
▸ Your feet should feel very flat on the floor, with your weight distributed evenly on the balls of your feet.
▸ Your knees should feel flexible and never locked.
▸ You should have a feeling of lift, or buoyancy, from your pelvis to the top of your head. (We need to lift *away* from gravity rather than giving in to it.) To achieve this feeling easily, lift your hands above your head, stretching upward, and slowly lower your hands to the side while keeping the stretch feeling. You should feel this expansion and lift between the waistline and your two bottom ribs, the floating ribs.
▸ If you are lifting properly, your chest will feel high and your ribs will feel open and expanded, establishing a comfortable and buoyant position. Some teachers use the visual image of a string lifting the chest as one sings. Another helpful suggestion is to imagine the joint at the top of your spine (it sits between the ears and behind the eyes) lifting up to the ceiling as your spine relaxes downward into your tailbone.
▸ Your shoulders should be relaxed and down, not rolled too far back, and certainly not rolled forward. Relax them in the center and let your shoulders float on your ribcage.
▸ Your arms are relaxed by the side and bent a bit at the elbows. Keep your hands relaxed. If you feel that you move your hands or fingers too much, try lightly placing your fingertips on your sides. This is a better option than moving your fingers in a nervous manner when performing, which can distract the audience from your beautiful sounds.
▸ Your neck should feel long and open all around.
▸ Your head should feel suspended and not jut forward. Look straight ahead. Some teachers also use the imagery of a string lifting from the middle of the head.

Correct Body Alignment—Sitting (Track 4)

During choral rehearsals, you may be singing while seated a majority of the time. Find a chair at home that most closely resembles the type of chair used in rehearsals. Heavily padded chairs or the sofa will not do.

Standing directly in front of the chair, stretch your hands high in the air, slowly lowering them to your sides. The chest should feel higher and the ribs out. Remember to maintain the feeling of lift out of the pelvis. Let the shoulders float on the ribcage. Your neck should feel long and open all around. Your head should feel suspended in the middle by a string.

Very slowly seat yourself on the front half of your chair while maintaining the lift in the upper body. Do not collapse as you sit. Remember to allow the joint at the top of the spine that sits between the ears and behind the eyes to lift up to the ceiling as the spine relaxes downward into the tailbone.

Figure 3.2 Correct Body Alignment—Standing

Your back should not touch the back of the chair. If you have back problems and need the support of the chair back, sit as tall as possible. Place your feet flat on the floor, slightly apart. You should feel a lift out of the chair.

Remember, to produce the best possible sound, you must always sit like a pro during rehearsals (see figure 3.3).

Figure 3.3 Correct Body Alignment—Sitting

Holding a Choral Folder or Music

When holding a choral folder or music during practice sessions, rehearsals, or a performance, set the body alignment first, then set the folder in line with the body. Singers often tend to position their bodies around the choral folder, rather than placing the folder in line with their bodies. The folder should be held high enough so that you can see both the music and the conductor (see figure 3.4). If you are looking down at the music, you are placing pressure on the vocal instrument. Remember to look straight ahead. Glance down at the music, when necessary, only with your eyes. Keep your shoulders down and relaxed and your back open.

Figure 3.4 Correct Body Alignment—Holding a Choral Folder

Figure 3.5 Correct Body Alignment—Using a Music Stand

Using a Music Stand

It is acceptable to use a stand during practice sessions as long as the stand is placed at the same level as where the folder will eventually be held (see figure 3.5). Again, you should not have to look down to read the music. If you are tall, use books or a platform to bring the stand up to the desired height.

BREATH

If the body is the vessel, the breath is the motor of the voice. Only when correct body alignment has been established will the breath enter easily without creating unwanted tension. Do not begin to sing without preparing the body and breath for singing. Not only is it a waste of your time, but you will find that you pay for it in the end, as your voice will tend to become quickly fatigued. In addition, singing or speaking without a supported breath may cause a number of other vocal problems, including irritation, sore throat, and in the worst case, nodules.

The main muscle of *inspiration* (breathing in) is the diaphragm. When the brain gives the impulse for breath, the diaphragm descends, enlarging the chest cavity, which creates a vacuum that draws air into the lungs (see figure 3.6). The lower abdominal muscles are the muscles of *expiration* (breathing out). The resistance of the lower abdominal muscles against the contracted diaphragm controls the amount of airflow to the vocal cords (see figure 3.7). It is important to note that the diaphragm does not support the tone; it keeps the tone steady.

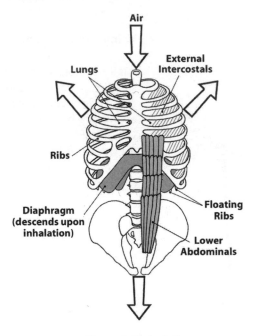

Figure 3.6 Inhalation

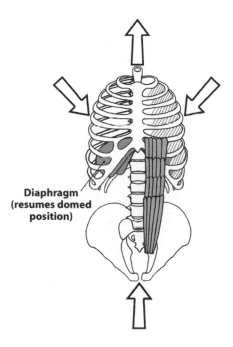

Figure 3.7 Exhalation

**Diaphragm
(resumes domed
position)**

For the breath to enter the body without restriction, space must be created. You may have been asked in the past to raise the soft palate as you sing or to drop your jaw. Telling a singer to "drop the jaw" can be a very misleading direction from a voice teacher or conductor, and here's why: When someone is asked to drop his or her jaw, the usual response is to open the front of the mouth more. This action causes the jaw to jut forward and increases tension at the temporomandibular joints (TMJs), the joints of the jawbone and skull, which are located in front of the ears on both sides. Although a singer may have more space in the front by dropping the jaw, the soft palate is probably not raised, and the throat is likely tensing to lift it, rather than relaxing.

The jaw should swing down and back a little with one simple movement of the TMJs. To experience what this feels like, place the index finger of each hand just in front of the ears on both sides and move them forward until you locate the TMJs (see Figure 3.8). With your fingers on the TMJs, open the space as if you are about to yawn (a half yawn), but keep the tongue relaxed forward with the tip behind the lower teeth as you do.

Open and close the jaw several times to get used to this new sensation of swinging the jaw. You will feel a little "cave" at the TMJs as the jaw drops. This cave space is an indication that you are creating the space necessary for singing. The combination of the relaxed jaw, forward tongue, and the half-yawn space (cave) will allow the breath to move freely into the body.

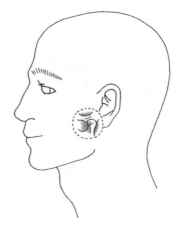

Figure 3.8 Temporomandibular Joints (TMJs) (Left View)

Before we move into the breathing exercises, here is a clarification of another misleading direction often given to singers, which is telling them to "take a breath." When singers "take" a breath, they usually do so by trying to pull as much air into the body as possible. This can produce an audible gasp and create tension in the body before the first note is produced. As a result, the sound will also be tense. As a singer, you want to "invite" the breath into your body and allow it to enter through an open space created by the swinging action of the jaw and the half yawn described above. When the body is fully open, the breath will be silent.

The way we breathe determines where the voice "goes." We take in food and sing through two different passageways in the throat. The trachea, in front, is used to move air in and out for singing or speaking, and the esophagus—the food tube—lies behind the trachea. Because the larynx (figure 3.11) is located at the top of the trachea, it is important to guide the breath through the trachea rather than the esophagus. Unwanted tension is created when a singer tries to "sing" through the food passage in the back of the throat instead of the air passage in front. Therefore, guide the breath up, not down, as you receive air into the body (see figure 3.9). When properly done, the tone will begin on top with an easy "sigh" feeling. If not, the tone will begin in the throat, creating a tense sound and a noisy breath on inhalation. Make sure the tip of the tongue is behind the lower teeth as you inhale. The tongue should feel flat on the floor of the mouth, and the air should glide over the top of the tongue as it enters the body.

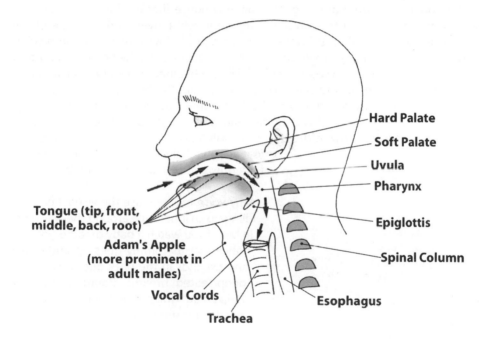

Figure 3.9 Parts of the Voice

BREATHING EXERCISES

 Breath Exercise 1: The Yawn Space (Track 5)

Exhale. Inhale through a very small mouth opening, like you are breathing in through a straw. It is important to breathe through the mouth to establish an open space (raised soft palate) in the back of the throat. Notice that the breath feels most prominent in the upper torso. Remember to guide the breath up, not down, and keep the tongue forward and relaxed. You will feel a cool swirl of air in the front of the mouth. Now, inhale through a midsized opening. You will now notice that the breath moves a bit lower in the body, around the navel and the cool swirl moves to the middle of the mouth. Now, place your thumbs in the fleshy area just below your ribs on both sides. Breath moves into the body in a wavelike motion. It does not fill the body from bottom to top. Next, inhale through a space that feels like the beginning of a yawn, an *ah* space. Remember to allow the jaw to swing down easily from the hinges on each side and keep the shoulders relaxed and down. Feel the breath fill to the side walls of the body, where your thumbs are located. The thumbs will move slightly outward. You will notice that the breath sits very low in the body. You will feel a cool spot in the back of the throat as you inhale. There will also be a feeling of openness and expansion in your back.

There should be no sound when you inhale. A gasp heard during the intake of air means there is closure and resistance in the throat. Have you ever heard a choral group gasp for air at the end of a phrase or during a very soft section of the music? This can really spoil the magic of the moment!

Many voice teachers use the visual image of filling up an inner tube around the waistline. In fact, if you watch a baby breathe, you will notice that its tummy goes up and down and expands in the back due to very low, deep-seated breaths. Breath Exercise 1 helps you grasp the feeling of depth needed for supported singing.

Remember to keep your chest high, ribs expanded, and shoulders relaxed at all times.

 Breath Exercise 2: The "Slow Leak" (Track 6)

This exercise, called the "slow leak," is a wonderful exercise for singers of all ages. It is especially beneficial for older singers who have lost control of their vibrato. The slow-leak exercise helps you pace your breath and gain more control over the lower musculature, which aids in the production of a sound with a more controlled vibrato. If your vibrato is too wide or too fast, practice this exercise daily.

Place one hand on your lower abdominals, just below the belt line. If you are not sure where your lower abdominals are, lie down on the floor and, keeping your legs together, lift them about six inches off the ground. You will definitely feel the lower abdominals tighten if you are not accustomed to using these muscles regularly.

Exhale on a "hissing" sound. It will sound like air leaking from a tire. Gently pull in the lower abdominals throughout the exercise. However, do not feel as if the body deflates during exhalation. Keep the ribs out, chest high, and back expanded. Stay open. The lower abs will move up and in to sustain the musical phrase and to provide support for accents, crescendos, and crisp consonants. The lower abs must always be active.

Inhale again to a count of 2, remembering to inhale through the yawn space (*ah* breath) and to send the breath to the side walls as you did in Breath Exercise 1. This time, exhale to a count of 8. As you become more proficient with the exercise, extend the count to 12, 16, and beyond, and reduce the intake count to 1 beat. However, do not try to take in too much air, as the lungs will feel "crowded." As you become more experienced through practice with the proper breathing habits for singing, the amount of air needed to complete a musical phrase will become clear.

The slow-leak exercise is great for developing a consistent legato sound, and you will begin to develop more dexterity for extended musical phrases.

You are now setting the stage for a much more enjoyable singing experience. In singing, nothing happens without breath, and nothing happens easily without support you can count on. As you practice these exercises on a regular basis, you will build trust in your breath for singing, a trust that you will be able to call on again and again in the future.

Tip

One of the most beneficial by-products of a concentrated, low breath is that the heart rate slows, which increases relaxation and creates a sense of ease in the body. This feeling of relaxation also helps calm your nerves during a choral audition or choral performance.

Breath Exercise 3: Pulse and the Activation of the Diaphragm (Track 7)

Have you ever noticed how a dog pants after a long walk or heavy play? We can learn from our canine friends. Pant like a dog. Go ahead, stick your tongue out. Place one hand on the belt line to make sure the breath is low enough.

Now, try panting with the tongue inside the mouth and relaxed forward *without* inhaling. On each exhalation, you will notice a feeling of pulse at the level of the lower abdominals. This pulse is the action we will use for all accents, to reinforce crisp consonants, and for staccato singing.

Place your thumbs on each side in the fleshy area just under the ribs. Now, with the feeling of pulse from the panting exercise, try the exercise in figure 3.10, repeating it on each of the consonants as indicated.

[tʃ] ch   [k]

[f]   [t]

Figure 3.10 Breath Exercise 3

If you have performed this exercise correctly, you should feel your thumbs push out slightly as each consonant is sounded. We are using the thumbs to feel the activation of the diaphragm. It is helpful to think of the diaphragm as a trampoline that completely bisects the torso. The combination of the pulse breath from the lower abdominals and the activation of the diaphragm (trampoline) felt by the thumbs is what allows a singer to perform crisp consonants, execute accents with ease, and sing staccato with energy—but without allowing the sound to be caught in the throat.

Breath Exercise 4: The "Surprise" Breath

One of the most difficult breaths for singers is the so-called catch breath. Part of the problem is in the name. If you think you have to "catch" your breath when a quick breath is needed to complete the musical phrase, you will tend to gasp. Since gasping usually indicates that we're horrified about something—therefore tense—this does not help with facial expression, either. A better description would be a "surprise" breath. When we are pleasantly surprised, our faces and bodies both tend to be more relaxed.

To avoid having to unlearn gasping, slowly rehearse passages where a surprise breath is required. Suspend the tempo of the passage you are working on as an exercise, open the body for a deep-seated breath, and finish the phrase. As you practice over time, allow the length of inhalation to become shorter and shorter until you have perfected a quick breath that allows you to remain open and complete the phrase with intensity. Again, the body must be trained to open for the breath and remain open throughout the act of singing.

Tip

If you run out of air before the end of the phrase, start at the end of the phrase and work backward a few notes at a time. As you do this, your muscles will be trained to react to the feeling of having more air and will not tighten at the end of the phrase. Do not reinforce tension or a collapsed chest at the end of the phrase by repeating an unsuccessful maneuver several times. Instead, change the rehearsal procedure immediately.

THE VOCAL SOUND

Now that you are on the way to better alignment and breathing habits, let's add sound. A choral ensemble must first produce a wonderful sound, and this wonderful sound is the result of beautiful individual voices working together. Perhaps you can recall an experience at a concert where a group was not producing a great tone. How did this make you feel? Maybe you were not aware of the exact problem but felt a sense of discomfort during the performance. Poor tone production not only affects the overall sound of the group, but also makes the musicality and technicality needed for great music making practically impossible.

On the other hand, you have undoubtedly heard many fine groups in the past that produced a marvelous sound, a sound that was thrilling because every singer was committed to producing a beautiful individual tone. This is the commitment asked of you: produce a beautiful tone on every single note, without exception. To commit to this, you must be able to recognize beautiful tone and repeat it over and over again. Music requires listening, and we must always listen as we sing. When you are singing well, ask yourself this question: What was I thinking and doing to bring about this result?

A beautiful tone is free, buoyant, resonant, warm, energetic, exciting, engaging, supported, inspiring, and capable of agility and dynamic change. A beautiful tone is created from the combination of yawn (cave space) and sigh, and a purely produced vowel sound, followed by pacing the breath and the phrase with the lower abdominals. The yawn feeling naturally lowers the larynx into the most favorable, relaxed position for singing. The sigh creates the feeling of starting the tone above the bridge of the nose and gives the tone a beautiful "ring."

Try this exercise. Place either hand on your larynx. Yawn. If you allow the air to fall into an open body through the yawn space, the larynx (see figure 3.11) will lower naturally as you inhale. Now, with the hand still on your larynx, swallow. The larynx lifts as we swallow. Since we spend more time drinking or eating than yawning, the muscles that lift the larynx get more use than the muscles that lower the larynx. The challenge for singers is to maintain an open space so that the larynx will remain in a low position throughout the act of singing. Any closure at the onset of the sound will cause the larynx to rise. The larynx will move up at times, especially on higher tones, but only by a fraction of an inch. We are trying to avoid a sudden jolt caused by closure or pressure in the throat. The sigh must be released through the same space the air passed through during inhalation.

We get into trouble in upper tones because the larynx tends to "jam," especially on the note that comes just before the high note. Place more yawn on the notes *before* the higher tone to keep the larynx relaxed and down.

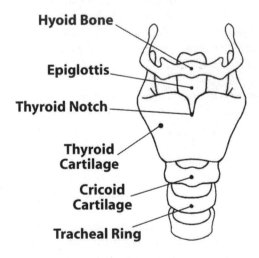

Figure 3.11 The Larynx—Front View

THE VOCAL CORDS

The vocal cords sit horizontally behind the Adam's apple. In singing, as you exhale and your diaphragm ascends, the air pressure against your vocal cords causes them to vibrate. The wavelike motion of the vibrating vocal cords creates a series of sound waves (pitches) that are picked up by a listener's ear.

The vocal cords (see figure 3.12) open in a triangular manner during breathing (1). To produce a lower singing tone, the triangle closes and the entire length of the vocal cords vibrates (2). The front of the cords vibrates for middle tones (3), and the back of the cords vibrates for higher tones (4).

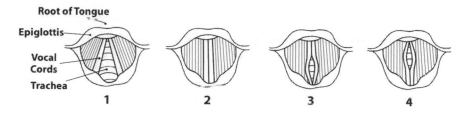

Figure 3.12 The Vocal Cords—Top View

A smooth onset of sound through the feeling of "sigh" is key to maintaining healthy cords. A harsh onset, called a glottal attack, will cause vocal cord fatigue and irritation. A singer who experiences a "scratchy" throat after singing should especially be mindful of this.

In addition, to produce musical tones, the vocal cords move together hundreds of times per second for middle tones and more than a thousand times per second on the highest tones in the female voice. During a three-minute choral piece or vocal solo, the cords will have closed (adduction) and opened (abduction) about 200,000 times or more for women, and perhaps half that number for men.

To view pictures of the vocal cords online, visit www.voicedoctor.net. This website also provides useful information about the voice in general.

VIBRATO

A natural, even vibrato adds warmth and "shimmer" to the sound. However, there are conductors who ask their singers to sing without vibrato. It is really up to the taste and training of the conductor. However, as one generic sound will not work for every piece of music in the vast choral repertoire, the final decision ideally should be based on the musical work to be performed.

Sound travels in waves. Vibrato is an oscillation of pitch that moves above and below the pitch in a wavelike motion. An even vibrato is heard at the rate of about 5 to 7 vibrations per second (see figure 3.13).

Figure 3.13 Vibrato

An out-of-control vibrato will destroy the choral sound, as the pitch will become easily distorted. If you feel your vibrato is too wide or too fast, work with the breathing exercises, especially Breath Exercise 2, as a first course of action. Make sure to use the lower abdominals to energize the phrase as you sing. If you continue to struggle, consult a private teacher. A natural, even vibrato should result from the yawn-sigh combination and the pacing of the breath.

THE RECIPE FOR BEAUTIFUL SINGING

What follows is the recipe for beautiful singing:

▶ Alignment
▶ "Visualizing" or hearing in your mind a beautiful sound
▶ Creating a yawn space with the tongue relaxed forward
▶ Inhalation—inviting the breath and guiding it up through the *ah* space and over the tongue

▸ Releasing the purely produced
vowel sound through a sigh, which
will create an easy onset and carry
the tone forward
▸ Phrasing with the lower abdominals
while keeping the body open—chest
high, ribs out, and shoulders relaxed

This process is repeated for every phrase we
sing. Practice it until it becomes second nature.

> **Tip**
>
> An easy release is just as important as an easy onset of tone. To stop a sound, simply stop the airflow while the space is still open or inhale through an open space to renew the breath for the next phrase. Do not close the rhroat to stop a sound.

VOCAL TECHNIQUE EXERCISES

There are a few dependable, focused vocal exercises that garner faster results. The powerful exercises that follow will help you to establish a daily warm-up routine in an order that most benefits your voice.

Before we begin singing, however, let's establish some basic guidelines to focus your practice and maximize the benefits you receive from your sessions. You will not be able to accomplish each of the guidelines in the first several sessions, but continued work will produce amazing results.

1. Rehearse in a location where you can make sound without feeling self-conscious about it. Singing to yourself will not help you learn to project the voice. When practicing, always sing to something, whether that something is a picture across the room or an imaginary audience. It is important to fully release the voice as you practice.
2. Alignment, then breath, then sound. Memorize the recipe for beautiful singing and practice it until it becomes second nature.
3. The goal of each practice session is to leave the session with one positive accomplishment.
4. If it hurts, stop! If you are feeling tightness or strain, check alignment and breath immediately.
5. Keep your entire body open and receptive when singing. In other words, open the space when you breathe and keep that space open throughout the act of singing. The tone has to gain access to the resonators, so do not block it.

6. Every vowel must be tall inside the mouth. Feel the molars separate in the back. Remember to open the space by allowing the hinges to swing on both sides. Vowel shape combined with proper breath support will result in a great tone. Since many of us speak with little mouth movement, this will take a bit of practice, but the work will be well worth the effort. Keep the tongue relaxed forward.

7. The vowel shape is always vertical, never horizontal. A horizontal shape creates a terrible, spread sound. Breathe the vowel and wrap the lips around the vowel to create a warm sound. This was called the "fishmouth" by the late Frauke Haasemann, a pioneer in the field of group vocal technique.

8. As you sing lower, lighten the sound. Do not push into the lower register. Lift the sound on descending scales. Keeping the facial space open (cheeks high and nose flaps open) will help to keep the sound placed correctly on descending scales. Always lift, never press. The sound should move behind the eye sockets and toward the two upper teeth.

9. The exercises are structured to include all voice parts. If an exercise becomes too high or too low, do not strain to sing the notes. Simply sing up or down the octave or wait until the piano accompaniment reaches a range that is more comfortable for you.

10. There is never a glottal attack (hard attack). A glottal attack is heard as a "pop" at the beginning of a tone. This is not only harmful to the vocal cords, but it is damaging to the sound of a group. An easy onset through the feeling of sigh is recommended for a clean attack.

11. If your practice session is not going well—and this does happen from time to time—sing the one piece you always sing well to get yourself into a better frame of mind. Also, you may want to figure out why this piece works for you when others do not.

12. Try to set up a regular practice session. Practice sessions should ideally be 30 minutes for adults and 20 minutes for children. A focused practice session for 30 minutes is better than one hour of unfocused practice.

13. Sing with the entire body engaged at all times. You should feel free to use your hands to direct sound as you practice. Get the whole body involved in the sound.

For each vocal exercise, directions for performing the exercise and the benefits to be gained are provided. It is very important for you to understand why you are working on a particular exercise. Additional tips and reminders will be reinforced on the CD. The exercises become more challenging as you go along. Do not try to do all exercises in one sitting if you are a beginner. Do not underestimate the importance of these first exercises, as they are the cornerstones of a solid vocal technique.

Vocal Exercise 1: Sigh—Middle to Low Range (Track 8)

Directions: In the middle part of your range, sigh slowly on an [i] *ee*. Initiate the sound from the lower abdominals and pull them gently up and in throughout the sound. Feel as if the sound starts at the bridge of the nose. Relax the tongue forward. As the pitch descends, do not allow the sound to fall into the throat, keep directing it into the cheekbones. Keep the ribs out, chest high, and shoulders relaxed. Sigh again on an [u] *oo* in the middle of the range. Allow the lower abdominals and breath to do the work. Do not lean into the sound from the chest or drop the chin as the pitch descends. Look straight ahead.

[i] ee

[u] oo

Benefit: The sigh relaxes the air and provides an easy onset at the beginning of each tone. A slow sigh combined with a focused and forward vowel sound from an upper note to a lower note helps to connect the upper and lower areas of the voice so that a change in registration is unnoticeable.

Tip

There is a tendency to lower the chin as we descend in pitch and raise the chin as we ascend. Keep looking straight ahead and do not try to manipulate the sound by moving the head. Trust your breath.

Vocal Exercise 2: Connecting the Sigh to Pitch—Descending Triads (Track 9)

Directions: First sigh, and then immediately sing the descending triad connecting the sigh to the notes. We will sigh before every repetition, and the pitch of the sigh should be just slightly higher than the first note of each repetition. Be sure to maintain the intensity of the final note until the rest. Renew the breath on the rest through an open space for the next set. Breathe the vowel sound. Use the lower abdominals to maintain an energized sound. Remember to allow the lower abdominals to spring out on the next breath in order for them to move inward again for the new phrase beginning. The notes should feel just as easy as the sigh.

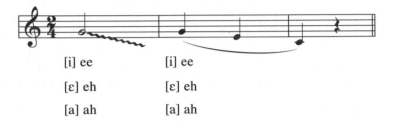

[i] ee   [i] ee

[ɛ] eh   [ɛ] eh

[a] ah   [a] ah

Benefit: The sigh relaxes the sound. The exercise begins to establish the yawn-sigh connection to each tone. In addition, rhythmic breathing in the exercise will provide the foundation for phrasing. Finally, this exercise helps to connect the middle and lower voice.

 Vocal Exercise 3: Hung–ah (Track 10)

Directions: The back of the tongue will lift against the soft palate for this exercise. Maintain an *ah* space (yawn space) inside and allow the humming sound of the *ng* to resonate fully. To release the sound, lower the back of the tongue quickly. The jaw should move only slightly, as it should already be in a lowered position for the *ah* (yawn) space.

Hung   [a] ah

              [o] oh

              [ɛ] eh

Benefit: This exercise increases resonance and ring in the voice and helps you to avoid nasality in the sound.

Vocal Exercise 4: Glissando—Fifth (Track 11)

Directions: Now, let's work on the sigh starting with a lower note and moving to a higher note. You should feel the sound start at the bridge of your nose and behind the eye sockets. Retain the pure vowel sound throughout the exercise and maintain the yawn feeling on the upper tone. Be sure to glissando (slide) from pitch to pitch by intensifying the vowel and using the lower abdominals to pace the breath. Renew the breath at the end of each phrase through an open space. Breathe the vowel sound.

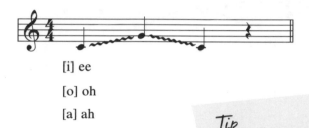

[i] ee

[o] oh

[a] ah

Benefit: You will connect the lower voice to the middle voice, smoothing out the registers. This exercises establishes the yawn feeling needed for higher tones and increases resonance and focus in the voice.

Vocal Exercise 5: Ascending Triads (Track 12)

Directions: Use the lower sigh established in Vocal Exercise 4 to perform these ascending triads. Maintain a forward placement on the lower tones (behind the eye sockets) and open the space on the upper tones.

> **Tip**
>
> The bright vowels, [i] *ee* and [ɛ] *eh*, must be felt high in the cheekbones with plenty of space between the tongue and the roof of the mouth. You will need a relaxed upper lip and relaxed tongue, as the tongue tends to pull back on these vowels. The tip of the tongue should relax behind the lower teeth.

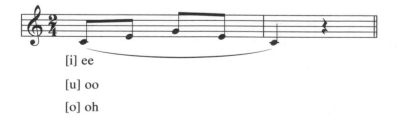

[i] ee

[u] oo

[o] oh

Benefit: This exercise further refines the benefits in Vocal Exercise 4.

 Vocal Exercise 6: Glissando—Octave (Track 13)

Directions: Same as Vocal Exercise 4. Remember to always focus the sound behind the eye sockets as you descend. Feel the sound move forward toward the upper teeth for maximum resonance.

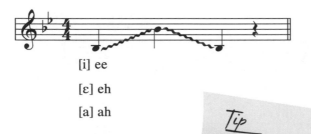

[i] ee

[ɛ] eh

[a] ah

Benefit: You will connect the lower voice to the higher voice, smoothing out the registers. This exercise establishes the yawn feeling needed for higher tones and increases resonance and focus in the voice.

Tip

If you think your tone is nasal, hold your nose as you sing. If the sound is in the nose, you will know it immediately. If you can sing the tone while the nose is held, the sound is balanced correctly. We absolutely want nasal resonance, but we do not want the tone completely in the nose.

 Vocal Exercise 7: Range Extension—Octave (Track 14)

Directions: Use the technique established in Vocal Exercise 6 to perform this exercise. Maintain a forward placement on the lower tones (behind the eye sockets) and open the space on the upper tones.

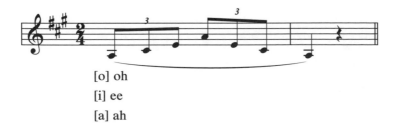

[o] oh
[i] ee
[a] ah

Benefit: You will connect the lower voice to the higher voice and extend the range up and down. This exercise establishes the yawn feeling needed for higher tones and increases resonance and focus in the voice.

 Vocal Exercise 8: Legato and Staccato (Track 15)

Directions: Remember to gently pull the lower abdominals up and in as you sing this exercise. You should feel a light bounce in the diaphragm on the staccato notes initiated by the pulse of the lower abdominals to avoid singing them in the throat (see Breath Exercise 3). Do not make the staccato notes too short, and listen carefully to pitch. Make sure to sing the staccato pitches directly in the center of the pitch. Think open space (yawn) before the higher tone to avoid "jamming" the sound.

[sa] sah	[sa] sah
[fa] fah	[fa] fah
[ta] tah	[ta] tah

Benefit: This exercise coordinates the abdominals and relaxed tongue with consonants for a more forward sound. You will learn to sing staccato with ease and intensity.

 Vocal Exercise 9: Five Vowels (Track 16)

Directions: Prepare the higher tone at the onset of the sound. Sigh the entire exercise. Yawn the upper tones, and gently pull in the lower abdominals as you sing. Round lips on the higher tones will keep the sound from spreading. The tone should feel forward and high in the cheekbones as you descend in pitch. Lift the lower tones so the pitch does not *flat* on the way down. Then, reverse the order of the vowel sounds.

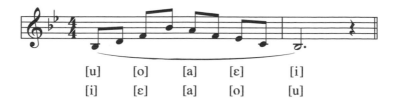

| [u] | [o] | [a] | [ɛ] | [i] |
| [i] | [ɛ] | [a] | [o] | [u] |

Benefit: This exercise helps to increase the higher range of the voice from bottom to top. Intonation on the descending pitches will be improved. You will learn to produce uniform vowel sounds on all vowels throughout the range.

 Vocal Exercise 10: Agility (Track 17)

Directions: As in the exercise above, prepare the higher tone as you breathe for the first note. Yawn the upper tone, and pace the breath with the lower abdominals. Remember to focus the vowel forward as you descend in pitch. Keep the pace steady, as there is a tendency to rush. As you progress, choose your own vowel combinations or sing the exercise on a single vowel.

[i]   [o]
[ɛ]   [a]
[o]   [a]

Benefit: This exercise increases the higher range and agility of the voice and connects the range from top to bottom.

Tip

Do not add *h*'s in melismatic singing—many notes to one vowel, as in Vocal Exercise 10. It wastes air and takes focus away from the sound. Re-sing and renew the vowel on each note instead. "Play" the notes in front of your eyes or draw the notes in the air while you practice to coordinate the voice with the brain. As a rule, the more notes on the page, the lighter you sing for clarity of pitch.

VOCAL MUSICIANSHIP EXERCISES

Many singers are not equipped with the full array of vocal tools to perform musically. How many times have we been told in a rehearsal, "Crescendo!" or "There is an accent on that note!" We try to deliver what the music calls for, but are unsuccessful much of the time because we have not learned how to vocally produce these requests.

After you have warmed up the voice with the exercises above, spend a few minutes at the end of each practice session working to improve your musicality. As you become more proficient with these vocal musicianship exercises, begin to incorporate them into the vocal technique exercises above to improve your overall musicianship. Be creative with these, and always sing every note musically. Try the exercises without the CD (*a cappella*) once you have mastered the exercise with the CD. Be sure to always listen as you sing.

Intonation

Believe it or not, you have control over your pitch to a great degree. Flatting tends to occur most often on longer final pitches, repeated pitches, and on half steps (especially descending), so we will focus on these areas in the exercises below.

Vocal Musicianship Exercise 1: Energizing Tone and Pitch (Track 18)

Directions: Energize the sound all the way to the end with the support of the lower abdominals for 7 beats. Feel as if the pitch lifts all the way to the end of the tone. To help maintain the intensity, please the index finger of one hand at the level of the ear pointing out. As you sing the exercise, extend the arm out and up slowly as if the index finger is slowly riding up an escalator. This action will reinforce the lift needed to improve the pitch and intensity of the tone. Remember to maintain the focus of the vowel.

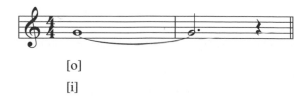

[o]

[i]

Benefit: This exercise helps you to improve intonation on longer tones through pacing the breath with the lower abdominals and lifting the sound.

Tip

Do not allow the sound to fade away on final notes. Keep the lower abdominals engaged until the very end of the sound to end the phrase with intensity.

 Vocal Musicianship Exercise 2: Repeated Pitches (Track 19)

Directions: Like the longer tone, repeated pitches tend to become lower and lower in pitch as they are sung. Repeated pitches should always lift. Use the index finger as you did in Vocal Musicianship Exercise 1 to reinforce a renewal of pitch on each tone. Gently pull in the lower abdominals to maintain focus in the sound. Energize the final note until the rest as in the exercise above. After you have mastered the exercise, reverse the direction of the vowels.

[vi]   [vɛ]   [va]   [vo]   [vu]

[vu]   [vo]   [va]   [vɛ]   [vi]

Benefit: This exercise helps to improve pitch on repeated tones using different vowel combinations. The exercise ends on a longer tone to reinforce the work in Vocal Musicianship Exercise 1.

 Vocal Musicianship Exercise 3: Chromatic Scale (Track 20)

The chromatic scale is made up of all the half steps within an octave (from c to c). A half step is the distance between adjacent keys on the piano (e.g., from c to c-sharp).

Directions: This exercise is performed with *solfeggio*, or *solfège*. A nonphonetic guide to pronunciation is included below. Note that the syllables change on the way down the scale. However, you may also choose to sing this exercise using a single vowel.

Place either hand at chest level in front of your body. As you sing, use the hand to imitate the size of each half step. Think bigger half steps on the way up and tiny half steps as you descend. Make sure to engage the breath throughout the exercise. Breathe every two measures. When you have mastered the exercise, sing it without the help of the CD to continue to perfect your pitch. Check your pitch using a piano or pitch pipe.

Solfège Pronunciation: doh, dee, reh, ree, mee, fah, fee, sol, see, lah, lee, tee, doh (ascending)
doh, tee, teh, lah, leh, sol, seh, fah, mee, meh, reh, rah, doh (descending)

The *r*'s are slightly flipped. Be sure to keep the *ah* sounds high and forward as you sing for better intonation.

Benefit: This exercise helps perfect intonation on ascending and descending half steps and to focus listening skills through the use of solfège.

Vocal Musicianship Exercise 4: Whole Tone Scale (Track 21)

The whole tone scale is a six-note scale made up entirely of whole steps. A whole step is an interval made up of two half steps (e.g., c to d on the piano keyboard).

Directions: Rehearse this exercise on an [a] *ah* vowel. As you sing this exercise, use the hand to imitate the size of the whole step as you did in the previous exercise. Think larger whole steps on the way up and smaller whole steps as you descend. Make sure to engage the breath throughout the exercise. When you have mastered the exercise, select other vowels and sing it without the help of the CD to continue to perfect your pitch.

[a]

Benefit: This exercise helps perfect intonation on ascending and descending whole steps and to focus listening skills.

Crescendo and Decrescendo

Vocal Musicianship Exercise 5: Crescendo (Track 22)

A crescendo means that the volume will gradually become louder as we sing. The symbol for a crescendo is included in the exercise, but often one will find *cresc.* in the musical score rather than the symbol. You should draw the symbol into your score so that the eyes see the marking clearly.

Directions: Intensifying the vowel and the upward and inward motion of the lower abdominals makes a crescendo. Begin the motion with less intensity at the beginning of the tone, and increase the intensity to increase the volume. Begin piano and crescendo to forte over 7 beats. The inward motion of the lower abdominals is very slow. Make sure not to deflate the body as you crescendo. Keep the body open and the ribs out as in all the other exercises.

[i]

[o]

Benefit: This exercise helps teach you to crescendo with intensity with the use of the lower abdominals rather than pressing with the throat.

 Vocal Musicianship Exercise 6: Decrescendo (Track 23)

As with the crescendo, one often finds *decresc.* in the musical score to indicate that the volume becomes gradually softer. It is more difficult to decrescendo than it is to crescendo, as the tendency in the decrescendo is to decrease the sound too quickly. This causes a lessening of intensity at the end of the tone, usually resulting with the sound locking in the throat.

Directions: Begin this exercise forte and decrescendo to piano over 7 beats. To make a decrescendo, the lower abdominals lessen in intensity as the volume softens. The volume must soften very slowly. *Slowly* is the key word here. As the sound softens, continue to focus the voice outward and keep the throat open. Find a place on the wall to sing to or use a finger to direct the sound forward as you soften. Soft singing is much like ventriloquism, in that we must continue to "throw" the voice forward as the sound becomes softer.

[a]

[o]

Benefit: This exercise helps you make an even decrescendo, ending the sound with intensity.

 Vocal Musicianship Exercise 7: *Messa di voce* (Track 24)

Whereas a crescendo or decrescendo may happen over a series of pitches, the *messa di voce*, or swell of the voice, is a crescendo followed by a decrescendo on one pitch. Messa di voce is used quite extensively in early music, but it can be found throughout the vocal literature.

Directions: This exercise will combine the directions for the crescendo and the decrescendo above. Increase the intensity of the lower abdominals for the crescendo and lessen the intensity while keeping the tone focused outward and throat open for the decrescendo. Begin piano, crescendo to mezzo forte, and decrescendo back down to piano over 6 beats.

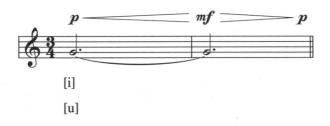

[i]

[u]

Benefit: This exercise is one of the most important development exercises for you. Phrases and single words or syllables will become more expressive musically once you have mastered this technique.

Articulation

Vocal Musicianship Exercise 8: Accents (Track 25)

There are many types of accents in music, ranging from very heavy accents to stress on a word or syllable. For any type of accent or marked singing (marcato), the pulse action in Breath Exercise 3 will be needed to keep the sound from originating in the throat.

Directions: To create an accent, a slight decay in sound must happen after the initial attack. However, keep the breath moving through the tone at all times. Use the pulse of the lower abdominals and the trampoline effect of the diaphragm to intensify the consonants in the exercise. Remember to pull in the lower abdominals gradually, not in a convulsing manner, and keep the body open (chest high, ribs out, and shoulders relaxed) and tall while singing. Let the breath do the work.

[va]

[dɛ]

[bi]

Benefit: You will learn to fully engage the body to produce powerful accents in music without allowing the sound to originate in the throat.

Vocal Musicianship Exercise 9: Staccato and Legato (Track 26)

Staccato singing is indicated by a dot above or below a note, telling you that the note is short. The danger in staccato singing is to sing the notes too short without energy, thus affecting the pitch. Like the accent, singers tend to squeeze the throat to produce an accent rather than using the breath to spark the sound.

Directions: You should feel each pitch "bounce" through the pulse of the lower abdominals. Keep the throat and body open during the exercise and the tongue relaxed forward. For the legato (smooth) part of the phrase, allow the lower abdominals to move in easily without the feeling of bounce needed for the staccato.

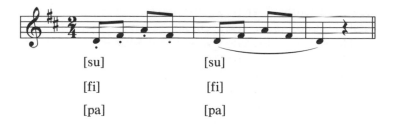

[su]   [su]

[fi]   [fi]

[pa]   [pa]

Benefit: You will learn to sing staccato notes in the center of the pitch with proper support. Staccato aids in the development of a consistent legato and reduces breathiness in the voice.

Congratulations! You made it to the end of the exercises. These exercises will pave the way to a more rewarding vocal experience. Through continued practice, you should reap remarkable benefits. Instead of leaving the choral rehearsal exhausted vocally, you will leave refreshed and energized.

CD TRACK LISTING

Track	Title	Time
1	Welcome and Instructions	2:22
2	Preparing the Body for Singing	3:04
3	Establishing Correct Body Alignment—Standing	1:52
4	Establishing Correct Body Alignment—Sitting	1:38
5	Breath Exercise 1: The Yawn Space	2:26
6	Breath Exercise 2: The "Slow Leak"	1:26
7	Breath Exercise 3: Pulse and the Activation of the Diaphragm	1:43
8	Vocal Exercise 1: Sigh—Middle to Low Range	1:12
9	Vocal Exercise 2: Connecting the Sigh to Pitch—Descending Triads	2:39
10	Vocal Exercise 3: Hung-ah	2:35
11	Vocal Exercise 4: Glissando—Fifth	2:26
12	Vocal Exercise 5: Ascending Triads	2:16
13	Vocal Exercise 6: Glissando—Octave	2:28
14	Vocal Exercise 7: Range Extension—Octave	2:52
15	Vocal Exercise 8: Legato and Staccato	1:48
16	Vocal Exercise 9: Five Vowels	5:30
17	Vocal Exercise 10: Agility	3:51
18	Vocal Musicianship Exercise 1: Energizing Tone and Pitch	1:45
19	Vocal Musicianship Exercise 2: Repeated Pitches	1:12
20	Vocal Musicianship Exercise 3: Chromatic Scale	1:44
21	Vocal Musicianship Exercise 4: Whole Tone Scale	1:01
22	Vocal Musicianship Exercise 5: Crescendo	1:03
23	Vocal Musicianship Exercise 6: Decrescendo	1:17
24	Vocal Musicianship Exercise 7: Messa di voce	1:14
25	Vocal Musicianship Exercise 8: Accents	1:37
26	Vocal Musicianship Exercise 9: Staccato and Legato	1:57
27	Closing Comments	:25

Total Time   **56:36**

CHAPTER

THE AUDITION: BEFORE, DURING, AND AFTER

ou have planned for a successful audition experience, gathered all the appropriate information, and prepared vocally and musically to the best of your ability. The next step is the actual audition.

ABOUT AUDITION ANXIETY

First, remember that choral groups advertise for new members because they need you. Second, know that the conductor wants you to be wonderful. Nervousness is natural during an audition because the body is flooded with adrenaline. Yet much of the anxiety a singer experiences during an audition may stem from lack of preparation. If you are adequately prepared and confident, you will have much less of the understandable anxiety associated with the audition process.

Singers sometimes suffer from serious performance anxiety, which can be crippling during an audition or a performance. There are many books about how to deal with performance anxiety and stage fright. You can find an extensive listing on Amazon.com under the subject heading "performance anxiety." Several of the titles are specific to the field of music.

Some choruses in your area may not require a full audition for membership. If you find yourself terrified at the very thought of auditioning, consider singing first in a nonauditioned ensemble to gain experience and build confidence in your musical abilities. A simple placement audition will most likely be required to determine your voice range and to ensure you can match pitch and meet the rehearsal and performance requirements.

As you prepare, visualize yourself as relaxed, yet confident during the audition. This exercise will help you create the best possible chance for your success.

GETTING READY

Before you leave your home, check again to be sure you have the following materials with you:

1. Directions and the contact number for the audition venue. It is also helpful to have the contact number of a member of the choral staff. Accidents, flat tires, and unforeseen traffic situations happen. Call a staff member immediately if you will be late for any reason.
2. The original score of the solo song in the key in which you will perform it.
3. A pencil for any last-minute notes or score markings.
4. Any paperwork required for the audition. To avoid unnecessary distraction, obtain and prepare these materials in advance, if possible.
5. A copy of your résumé, even if it is not packed with music credits. It is helpful to the conductor and music staff to know about your career path and skills.
6. Room temperature bottled water.

Dress appropriately for the audition. You will want to look your very best. Professional dress demonstrates to the conductor, staff, and volunteers that you are serious about becoming a singer in the chorus.

Before you walk out the door, spend at least 15 minutes warming up your body, mind, and voice. Warming up your voice in the car is not advisable. Do some stretching to wake up your body. Roll your shoulders. Roll your head from side to side. Be sure to breathe low in your body. Take a moment to go mentally through everything you have learned in your preparation for the audition. What is your solo piece about? What is the mood? How have your voice and sight-reading ability improved? Why would you like to sing in this particular chorus? Even if you ultimately are not selected, what would you like to learn from this audition experience?

These questions will help to focus your mind and attention. In addition, remember to take a few moments to acknowledge to yourself the good work and effort you have put forth in preparing for the audition.

Now use the CD to warm up your voice, and head out to the audition.

BEFORE THE AUDITION

Build in extra travel time, as you do not want the stress of running late to break your concentration in the audition room. However, try not to arrive too early, either, as a long wait may create additional, unneeded anxiety and tension.

On arrival, check in with the chorus representative, turn in any completed paperwork you have brought with you, and fill out any additional documents requested. Next, find a quiet place to relax and meditate for a moment. Some choruses provide a warm-up area. If so, use this space to do some breathing exercises (see Chapter 3) and vocal warm-ups and to focus your thoughts before singing for the conductor.

If you are able to meet with the accompanist prior to entering the audition room (a rare occurrence), set the tempo of the piece and sing through the music. Great accompanists—who are worth their weight in gold—usually do not require a lot of direction, as they are trained to follow the singer beautifully. However, if your accompanist for the audition is less experienced, point out repeats in the music, places where you will need more time for breath, and other interpretive suggestions as needed.

When the conductor is ready to see you, a representative from the chorus will call you into the audition room. Before you enter the room, take a slow, deep breath to clear your mind. Quickly review your answers to the questions from your warm-up at home. With these answers fresh in your mind, it is now up to you to go in and deliver an audition that will achieve your goal as a choral singer.

IN THE AUDITION ROOM

Enter the room with a smile and enthusiasm. A friendly "hello" is certainly welcome, and you will most likely be greeted in similar fashion. Keep in mind that the conductor may have already heard several auditions that day. It is up to you to perform an audition that will inspire and excite those who hear it. Do not, under any circumstances, walk into the room apologizing, whining about a cold, or complaining that you do not feel well. Singers are famous for this. Just go in and do your best. If you have a cold, it will be obvious to the conductor. It is much more impressive to those listening when a singer just walks into the room and delivers, cold or no cold. If you are feeling very ill, however, you will want to reschedule the audition.

Although it is important to be self-confident, do not walk into the room acting overconfident or cocky. You may have a great voice and read well, but if you are not a team player, the conductor may not consider you for the group. Everyone must work together in an ensemble; there is no room for prima donnas. Do what is asked of you during the audition. If you have a question or something is unclear, feel free to ask politely for clarification.

PERFORMANCE SUGGESTIONS

The conductor may ask a couple of questions to help you relax. However, if the schedule is very tight, you most likely will be expected to move right into the audition. Before you begin singing, check your body alignment. You should feel comfortable and natural, not rigid. If you wear glasses (especially large ones), you may wish to remove them for the solo piece. Make sure to keep your hair away from your face, as the conductor will want to see your facial expressions as you sing.

If the accompanist sets the tempo too fast or too slow, enter at the tempo you wish to use and the accompanist will follow. Take the lead and sing at the tempo that is comfortable for you. Do not try to conduct the accompanist. If a mistake occurs in the accompaniment, just keep going, and absolutely do not make a face. Focus on making your own beautiful sound and "selling the song." Energy placed elsewhere will take away from your performance.

As you sing, communicate the piece facially. Connect to your breath. Your hands should be relaxed and by your side unless there is an expressive gesture appropriate to the music. Resist the urge to fidget or make nervous movements while you are performing. Keep your shoulders relaxed. Do not judge or second-guess yourself as you sing.

This is *your* audition, so make the most of it. If you have thoroughly prepared, your "automatic pilot" will do the rest of the work for you. Be confident and musically spontaneous, and give it your best shot. Stay in the music, in the moment, and enjoy the experience. Perform your solo piece with clear intention, allowing the emotion of the music and your performance to shine.

Depending on the audition schedule and the length of your solo piece, the conductor may stop you during the performance. If so, do not take this as a bad sign. It simply means that the conductor either is so convinced of your musical abilities that he or she does not need to hear more, or is just trying to stay on schedule. As a common courtesy, conductors will generally let you know before the piece begins that they may stop you.

COMPLETING THE AUDITION

As you exit the room after singing, thank the conductor for hearing you. You have performed to the best of your ability at that moment. On your way out, do not make excuses at the door about how you sounded better in the warm up room or in the car on the way to the audition. Leave the room with a smile and appreciation, not complaints and apologies.

Some choruses require an interview or written exam as part of the audition process. This will generally take place after the sung portion of the audition. If you are interviewed, be as professional as possible and answer all questions to the best of your ability. Do not be afraid to ask questions as well. Engage in a conversation with the panel.

Sometimes a written exam is given to test a singer's knowledge of basic theory and musicianship. This is most common in auditions for professional ensembles. However, all singers can benefit from a review of the fundamentals of music. For more information, see Resource F: Online Choral Music Resources.

THE WAITING GAME

Results are usually not made available right after the audition. Some conductors believe in telling a singer immediately if he or she has been accepted into the ensemble.

In the majority of cases, however, the conductor will need time to reflect on the audition of each candidate before making a final decision.

Depending on the nature of the chorus, you may be requested to attend a callback, or second audition. The conductor may ask current chorus members, the assistant conductor, or a local voice teacher to attend the callback to provide further feedback. You may be given a piece of music and asked to prepare it for the callback. You may be asked to sing with a quartet of singers already in the ensemble, and you also may be required to sing your part of the work solo, so be sure to prepare thoroughly. Whatever the procedure, ask questions before the callback date if you are unclear about *anything*. At this point, the chorus is very interested in you. Go into the audition room and perform with the same musicality and enthusiasm that got you the callback in the first place.

If the chorus does not have callbacks, be patient. The conductor or a chorus representative will contact you as soon as a decision has been reached. In the meantime, audition for other choral groups. The more you audition, the more comfortable and experienced you will become with the process, which will increase your chances at getting into the chorus of your choice.

A Note to Parents

Encourage your child to sing, and help him or her prepare for auditions. Children's choruses tend to have several levels of choirs, usually ranging from a beginning chorus to an advanced group. The music staff will evaluate your child's musical abilities and place the child in the appropriate group. Although most parents would like to have their son or daughter placed in the most advanced group possible, the child's musical growth must take first priority. As your child's vocal and musical skills grow, he or she will be able to audition for placement in the more advanced groups.

THE AUDITION RESULTS

Audition results may be mailed to you or sent via e-mail, or a chorus representative or the conductor may contact you directly. For conductors, one of the most difficult parts of the job is deciding who gets in and who does not. However, it is up to the conductor to take into account the needs of the chorus and select the most appropriate singers to fill open positions in the group.

"SORRY, BETTER LUCK NEXT TIME"

Nobody likes rejection. It is disappointing and painful to learn that you did not make it despite all your hard work and preparation. However, it is not the end of the world, and it should not be the end of your growth as a singer. In fact, it is an opportunity to honestly assess your musical strengths and weaknesses and learn about which areas need further development.

If you are not accepted, call the music director or a staff member and ask for feedback about your audition. Say that you are interested in learning how you can improve for the next round of auditions. This will immediately gain you a lot of respect. Ask for specific suggestions. Use this information to focus your energies on strengthening your skills in those areas. This will pay off in the end by improving your performance in all your future auditions. However, do not call to whine about not being accepted or show disrespect to the conductor or music staff. If you want to sing in a group, you do not want to gain a reputation for being unpleasant or difficult.

If you are unable to get personal feedback, perform a self-evaluation of your audition experience. Review the following list of common reasons a singer is not accepted into a chorus.

1. Inadequate preparation (This should not be an issue for you if you prepared using the suggestions in this book.)
2. Too much vibrato or a tremolo (This will negatively affect the overall blend of the chorus.)
3. Tone quality needs improvement
4. Intonation needs improvement
5. Music-reading skills are not strong enough for the ensemble
6. Bad attitude

Continue working to master the areas where you need improvement, and keep trying. You will arrive at your next audition with more confidence, sharper skills, and a greater likelihood of success. Conductors are always delighted to see a singer return and give a better performance at the second audition. This level of commitment is inspiring to the music staff and paramount to the success of the choral ensemble.

A Note to Parents

Children today face so much rejection on a daily basis from other children, their parents, and their teachers. They often compare themselves to other children. This is especially challenging when a child's friends are accepted into a choral ensemble and he or she is not, particularly if it was the friend's encouragement that moved the child to audition in the first place. If your child was not accepted into the chorus, it is important that you provide the love and support needed to help him or her get through this time. Encourage your child to continue singing and to develop his or her own unique musical gifts.

"CONGRATULATIONS! YOU'RE IN THE CHORUS"

When you receive that letter or phone call saying you have been accepted into the chorus, celebrations are in order. You have just joined the ranks of millions of people around the world who regularly sing in choral groups.

If you have auditioned for and are accepted into more than one chorus, you have obviously prepared thoroughly and possess the skills necessary to make a positive contribution musically to an ensemble. You will now need to decide whether to sing in both groups or select the one ensemble that most closely suits your passion as a singer. According to Chorus America's (www.chorusamerica.org) recent study on choral singing, *America's Performing Art: A Study of Choruses, Choral Singers, and Their Impact*, 34% of choral singers belong to more than one group. However, before you make the final decision to join two choruses, be sure that you can keep the time commitments— including scheduled rehearsals and your own daily music practice and memorization sessions—of both organizations. If you are unable to sing with a group for any reason, notify the music director or audition coordinator as soon as possible to give a singer placed on the alternates list the opportunity to sing. Do not wait until the last minute to make your decision, as it will affect more than just you. The conductor will need time to make any adjustments necessary for the ensemble. However, if you decide to join later, you should expect to reaudition.

Once you are accepted, the chorus may send you a packet that includes the season calendar, rehearsal policies and procedures, tour information, and other important details about your obligations as a member. Professional singers will sign a contract for the season. Some choruses provide much of this information prior to the audition to help you identify potential conflicts and evaluate your ability to commit to the concert season.

Place all dates on your calendar as soon as you receive them. If the literature for the next concert has been finalized, ask the music librarian or conductor for the sheet music and a list of pieces to be prepared for the first rehearsal. You may be able to purchase your own copies, but be sure to purchase the same edition of the music that will be used in rehearsal. Begin learning the music well before rehearsals begin. Think how great it will feel to walk into the first rehearsal with your notes learned and ready to make music. You will make a great first impression, and the conductor will love you!

CHAPTER

THE REHEARSAL

 rehearsal is a practice session in preparation for a performance in front of an audience. Rehearsals are an exciting journey—a journey in which the ensemble re-creates, based on the interpretation of the conductor, the music of the great masters or composers of today. The number of choral rehearsals varies from group to group depending on the skill level of the singers and the difficulty of the literature. Professional choruses may have only four rehearsals to prepare for a major performance, whereas a community chorus or college ensemble may need 10 to 12 weeks.

To produce a top-notch concert, it is paramount that each singer attend rehearsals regularly. Every singer in the choral ensemble is an important part of the whole. The sound and overall morale of the group are negatively affected when singers miss rehearsals.

THE FIRST REHEARSAL OF THE SEASON

Prior to your first rehearsal as a new singer in an ensemble, you may receive a "welcome" phone call from your section leader, or you may be assigned a chorus buddy. Many choruses, especially large choruses, have a buddy system in place so that new members have a direct contact within the group. Your chorus buddy (or section leader) will introduce you to other singers in your section and keep you informed of chorus business during the first rehearsals. This is a wonderful way to get to know others in the group, especially for new members who are shy or feel too intimidated to initiate a conversation with others who have been in the chorus longer.

There may also be a new-member orientation prior to the start of the first rehearsal. The orientation will get you up to speed on the rules and regulations of the ensemble as well as provide information on tours, concert attire, dues, performances, and attendance policy.

Before heading out to your first rehearsal, be sure you have directions, the correct start time, and all the materials you will need. Try to arrive early. A late arrival to the first rehearsal will not make a good impression. Plan on traffic. If you must be late for any reason, call your section leader or appropriate chorus contact to let him or her know.

MATERIALS TO BRING TO EVERY REHEARSAL

Remember to bring a pencil or two to every rehearsal. The pencil is a key tool for the singer. Use it to mark problem areas to rehearse at home so that rehearsal time is not wasted. Throughout the rehearsal, the conductor will make suggestions for breath marks, tone quality, dynamics, diction, and phrasing. Each singer will need to mark his or her own score appropriately (see Chapter 6).

Life happens, and difficult situations may arise during the workday. As much as possible, "check your baggage" at the door. Let the rehearsal be a time of reconnection and centering. Come to the rehearsal with a positive attitude and enthusiasm for singing. This energy will keep you engaged throughout the rehearsal. A great conductor will inspire the singers in the rehearsal, but this energy must flow both ways. The singers feed off the energy of the conductor, and the conductor feeds off the energy of the chorus. Do not make the conductor drag you along; do your part to keep the rehearsal upbeat and exciting.

Some choruses distribute music to their singers prior to the beginning of the first rehearsal to give them an opportunity to rehearse before the first meeting. Once you receive your music, bring it with you always. Sharing music with your neighbor will result in misalignment of the body for each of you. In addition, important score markings will not be made in your own musical score.

Many churches and schools provide music folders for each singer. However, if you must purchase your own folder, which is usually the case in college, community, and professional choirs, the Black Folder, designed by Andrew Black, has been called "the world's best choral folder." You may order the folder directly from Andrew in Huntington Park, California, by calling (323) 588-9000 or online at www.emersonenterprises.com.

If bottled water is allowed in the rehearsal space, bring a bottle to rehearsal. You should drink as much water as possible throughout the day. The vocal folds are one of the last areas to receive the benefits of water. Depending on your build, most singers will need at least eight glasses or bottles of water each day. Singers with a smaller build will need less; singers with a larger build will need more. This intake does not include drinks that contain water such as tea, coffee, or soft drinks.

Although many singers record their private voice lessons, audiocassette recorders can be very distracting during the choral rehearsal. However, an audiocassette recorder can be a valuable learning tool for singers, especially those who do not read music well. Obtain permission to record the rehearsals from the conductor in advance. Purchase 120-minute tapes to avoid constant cassette changes. Be very mindful of the time, as you do not want to be disruptive to the conductor or your fellow singers.

THE REHEARSAL STRUCTURE

There are many ways to run a rehearsal, and every conductor is different. Rehearsal lengths vary according to the type of ensemble (college, community, or professional), the time needed to prepare for the concert, and the age group of the singers. Young children cannot rehearse productively for three hours, for instance. Many conductors use the following formulas for their rehearsal.

Example 1 (2- to 3-hour rehearsal)

▶ Most conductors include a warm-up period at the beginning of the rehearsal. The warm-up is very important, so do not miss it. A private warm-up before the rehearsal begins is also recommended. The conductor will begin to build the sound of the ensemble, a sense of intonation, rhythm, and sense of ensemble. The warm-up will prepare the singers vocally for the rehearsal ahead. Singers will need to connect to the singing voice versus the speaking voice they have used all day at work. If your conductor does not do warm-ups, plan to arrive early to warm up yourself. Do not risk hurting your voice by trying to sing without a proper warm-up.
▶ Rehearsal, Part 1: The group will rehearse two to three pieces or movements from a larger work. Generally, the conductor will begin with a more familiar piece right after the warm-up. Following the more familiar piece, the group will move directly into something new or more challenging. Because the singers feel "fresh" at the beginning of the rehearsal, this is the perfect time to introduce a more challenging piece.
▶ Announcements and a break will usually follow Part 1 of the rehearsal. The conductor, executive director, chorus president, or section leader usually makes the announcements. The break will normally last 10 to 12 minutes.
▶ Rehearsal, Part 2: Perhaps after a very brief warm-up to get the singers back into the singing voice, the chorus will rehearse a couple more pieces. The conductor may elect to continue work on the piece that was rehearsed before the break.

Example 2 (1 hour or less rehearsal)

▶ Warm-up.
▶ Rehearse two to four pieces. Depending on the situation, there may be announcements during this time, especially regarding performances, tours, or fundraising events in schools.

Example 2 is typical of a high school, middle school, or college choral rehearsal. Some select ensembles at the college level will rehearse three times per week for 1 1/2 hours. High school and middle school ensembles generally rehearse on a daily basis. Elementary school music may take place at 30-minute intervals either two or three times per week. Children's rehearsals are typically shorter, as children's voices tend to tire more easily. If the rehearsal is longer, more frequent breaks are usually needed to maintain focus and energy in the rehearsal.

RESPONSIBILITIES OF THE CONDUCTOR

The main responsibility of the conductor is to inspire the chorus to musical greatness in the rehearsals and performance. Sometimes the conductor is seen as the "bad guy," as it is he or she who is charged with maintaining order during the choral rehearsal. In addition, the conductor holds each singer accountable for learning the music and for missed rehearsals. The roles and responsibilities of the conductor vary from organization to organization, yet it involves much more than mere "hand waving." While the information below does not represent every situation, it should give you an idea as to the complexity of the conductor's role.

Prior to the beginning of the concert season, the conductor is hard at work selecting music and themes for the concerts, selecting the rehearsal and performance venues, planning the tour, and contracting instrumentalists and vocal soloists. In addition, the conductor will thoroughly analyze each piece of music to effectively communicate his or her interpretation of the music to the singers.

The summer months for leaders of community choruses will also include board meetings, fundraising activities, auditions for new singers, strategic planning with other chorus leaders, and development of the artistic vision. Conductors of school and community youth and children's choruses will work side-by-side with parents and administrators throughout the year.

Before the first rehearsal, the conductor will mail or e-mail singers important information about the upcoming season. The conductor, perhaps with the help of a volunteer, arrives early to set up for the rehearsal. During the rehearsals, the conductor offers expert teaching in vocal production, rhythm, intonation, phasing, foreign language pronunciation, poetic interpretation, and musical expression. He or she must deal with a variety of singer-related issues and questions. On an administrative level, the conductor acts as a creative problem solver with the board of directors or music staff in dealing with challenges that may arise during the season.

If the concert performance requires special lighting or staging, the conductor will work closely with a production committee to create the production flow for the event. This, of course, involves another series of meetings for planning and perhaps extra choral rehearsals when small groups are involved.

Prior to the performance, the conductor will rehearse with any guest artists and perhaps with an orchestra in some circumstances.

During the performance, he or she will act as the spokesperson for the chorus, but most important, will lead the musical forces in a first-class performance of each work prepared in rehearsals.

The job of conductor is a multifaceted endeavor. Many conductors hold full-time jobs in other disciplines while working part-time with a choral group. Understanding the many tasks the conductor must manage to effectively lead the chorus should be understood by each singer. Often, singers do not realize the incredible amount of work involved in taking on the responsibility as the conductor of a chorus. Perhaps a clearer understanding will help to foster mutual respect from singer to conductor and conductor to singer.

RESPONSIBILITIES OF THE SINGER

Sometimes singers place too much responsibility on the conductor. Part of this is because too many conductors hand-feed singers and do not train them to be interdependent in the ensemble. However, you are encouraged to think a bit differently, as the goal of this book is not just to help you get through the rehearsal but to teach you how to make every choral experience an incredible musical experience.

Conductors do not have an electronic mixing board on their stand to control every sound a singer makes. It is the responsibility of the conductor to lead the singers in the musical performance of a work; however, each singer must take responsibility for the musical direction the conductor provides during the rehearsal period. Marking the score and following those markings each and every time is crucial for great music making. Other general responsibilities include the following:

▸ *Coming to rehearsal with your notes and rhythms learned.* It is impossible to create art when the basic building blocks of music are not in place. Correct notes and rhythms are only the beginning of the music learning process and should be worked out individually prior to rehearsal. Solicit help from the section leader or conductor outside of rehearsal, if necessary.
▸ *Active listening.* If your voice quality is "sticking out," then you are not listening. Those with larger voices may be able to use only 70% to 80% of their voice in a choral setting. Those singers with lighter voices or the "blenders" may be able to use the full voice. If you are truly listening, the music will lead you to produce the appropriate sound.

▸ *A beautiful tone on every single note.* The conductor will prepare the sound according to the style of the piece. Once this is made clear, it is up to the singer to produce the sound over and over again.

▸ *Exact intonation on every note.* Believe it or not, you do have control over intonation. The conductor will provide help when needed to correct intonation problems, but you should listen carefully to self-correct as much as possible.

▸ *Beautiful phrasing.* Great phrasing is great music making, and it is up to you to maintain the integrity of the phrase each and every time.

▸ *Intelligible diction on each and every syllable.* The conductor or another singer will usually instruct the group in foreign language pronunciation. However, it is the responsibility of the singer to become an expert on the exact sound of each syllable of that language. Make sure you understand the proper translation of the text. Without an understanding of text, be it a foreign language or in your native tongue, the performance will be compromised and the audience will not understand the meaning of the piece.

▸ *To communicate the music through an engaged mind, body, and spirit.* You must become a reflection of the musical score.

▸ *To work as a team player with other members of your chorus to bring about a musical experience that you could not create alone.* Your voice should contribute to the sound of the whole, using your musical instincts to bring about the conductor's interpretation of the music.

Although this may seem like a lot to ask for, singers only have to prepare a single line of music in each work. Attention to the fine details in the music is the hallmark of a world-class chorus. Yes, the piece may be challenging, but you will be able to master your vocal part if you prepare the music in stages.

Contribute fully to the choral ensemble. Mere participation (i.e., just showing up and singing) is not enough. You must have courage to make mistakes and be responsible for them. Make the pencil your best friend in rehearsal. Avoid making the same mistake twice. Once an error is corrected, the conductor should not have to address it a second time.

Like the conductor, singers generally hold full-time jobs in addition to singing in a chorus. However, do not let the music suffer for lack of preparation. This can become a frustrating experience for you and for those singers who are prepared. Perhaps you will need to spend an hour or two each week in the beginning rehearsals until the notes and musical elements of the score are learned completely. If the conductor does not announce the pieces to be rehearsed at the next rehearsal, find out from him or her. Imagine how great you will feel when you are fully prepared at every rehearsal and ready to make beautiful music.

THE PROFESSIONAL SINGER

Many groups, especially church choirs, hire professional singers as section leaders in the choir. Although this can be a somewhat touchy situation, professional singers add another dimension to the group's musical experience in several ways. Volunteer singers may need to miss rehearsals due to a work commitment or holiday travel, yet paid singers are employed to attend every rehearsal on time, thus providing consistency in the ensemble. If a rehearsal must be missed due to another professional engagement, the arrangement for a substitute is usually required in church choirs.

The conductor is able to choose more challenging literature. The volunteer singers are provided with a professional model of sound and musicianship and will learn the music much faster. Paid singers most often really love their jobs and are quite helpful in leading and educating the volunteer singers. Of course, there can be the occasional prima donna who is just working for the paycheck. This type of professional singer can cause division and hurt feelings in the ensemble. However, this is often the exception rather than the rule. It is up to the conductor to choose appropriate singers and to dismiss a professional singer who is not a team player.

Although volunteer singers may be "forgiven" for lack of preparation in a rehearsal, professional singers are expected to produce exceptional results in an ensemble. Lack of preparation on the part of the professional singer, depending on the ensemble, may result in docked pay or loss of employment.

Some choruses may hire a professional core of singers, whereas other groups are fully professional ensembles. For information on professional singer compensation, see Resource J: Professional Singing Opportunities.

REHEARSAL TIPS

▸ Do exactly what the score says to do. Follow your markings each and every time. Conductors should not have to spend time in rehearsal stating the obvious, reminding singers to follow their markings. If the score says to crescendo, do it. This includes all new markings given by the conductor.
▸ Watch the conductor. Hold your music so you can see it and the conductor. You should be aware of the slightest change in gesture from the conductor. Set your posture first, and then place the music in its position. Do not gear the posture to the position of the music.

- Make sure your body is always in alignment when you sing. This will greatly affect your sound and energy in the rehearsal. This is very important during the learning process, as the muscles will memorize misalignment.
- If the chorus is seated for the rehearsal, sit on the front part of your chair. The upper part of the body should feel the same as if you are standing (see "Body Alignment" in Chapter 3). Feel "lift" out of the pelvis as you sit. Under no circumstances should you ever cross your legs while sitting.
- Be flexible. Be open and receptive to new ideas.
- Listen and respond appropriately to the sound of the group.
- If the chorus is reading through a piece of music for the first time:
  - Look first at the key and meter of the piece.
  - Read complete ideas and phrases rather than one note at a time.
  - Note any accidentals, key changes, meter changes, or repeat signs in the music.
  - Watch out for repeated notes; they are very easy to miss.
  - You may wish to tap lightly to maintain a steady pulse.
  - Sing musically always. If you make a mistake, keep going.
- Do not begin chatting with your neighbor when the conductor stops. Generally, when a conductor stops, it is to make a suggestion or correction. Pay attention all the time. If the conductor is working with another section, rest assured that most of the information provided to them will also apply to your section. Conductors and fellow chorus members find it very frustrating to repeat information that was just given to another section.
- Challenge yourself. Push the envelope musically without sticking out. This will help you to grow toward a rewarding performance.

ADDITIONAL GROUP REHEARSAL TIME

Many times, extra rehearsals will be called during a concert cycle. Full-group rehearsals such as chorus retreats or smaller section rehearsals will be scheduled to provide more time to master the literature for the concert. Chorus retreats are not only a wonderful time to get away to refine the music, but they are also an important time for the singers to bond. Section rehearsals also provide the singers with an opportunity to get to know one another better.

Depending on the type of group you sing in, there may be an opportunity to sing in a subgroup of the larger group. You may also have the opportunity to perform in a small group that is assembled to perform a single piece during the concert. This will further enhance your musical skills and will allow you to sing other styles of music that may not be appropriate for the larger group. Small group singing is an excellent way to increase your musical skills, as everyone has to carry his or her own weight in a small ensemble. Every leap forward musically is a benefit to the singer and to the whole group.

PRIVATE REHEARSAL: MAXIMIZING YOUR EFFORTS

Probably the most important rehearsal time is the private rehearsal, when each singer spends time perfecting his or her part outside of the rehearsal. Daily practice will increase the musical and vocal skills of the singer. As mentioned in Chapter 3, consistent practice is necessary so that the muscles of the body can perform the same functions over and over again.

Perhaps those sitting next to you will be encouraged to work harder. They will certainly notice your constant improvement and so will the conductor.

Find a comfortable place where you can make all kinds of sounds and not disturb family members or your neighbors. Always practice in a standing position (see Chapter 3). Use the CD or warm up with your own favorite exercises.

It is hoped that you have marked the score appropriately and indicated problem areas from rehearsal with a small "x" (see "General Markings" in Chapter 6). Locate the problem area, and work on that area of the music first. Do not waste time going over parts you already do well. Use your time efficiently by correcting the trouble areas in your part first. As you make corrections, erase the mark.

Some choruses provide learning CDs so that singers may learn their vocal parts outside of rehearsal. Although there are definite pros and cons, rehearsal CDs can be an easy tool for learning pitches in beginning rehearsals. However, the CDs are good for pitch learning only, as they do not indicate dynamic change nor do they contain text. In addition, the tempo included on the CD may or may not be the tempo that the conductor chooses.

Break down the music into layers, using the song-learning process from Chapter 2. You may want to record your private practice sessions for feedback. It may be uncomfortable at first, but the cassette recorder does not lie. You will become your own teacher.

Practicing while driving in a car is not recommended. Although you may think it is time well spent, the breath is not centered when you are trying to drive and sing at the same time. Body alignment is not upright while driving, and the muscles will once again memorize the misalignment.

Recordings can be a wonderful resource *after* the piece is learned. Remember, though, that a recording of a musical work may not represent the same interpretation, tempo, and sound ideal that your conductor has in mind. You do not want to learn other conductors' interpretations, nor would you want to bring those to your chorus rehearsal.

REHEARSAL SOCIALS

After you have done your homework in your private rehearsals, you may wish to schedule time with other chorus members to rehearse at your home. Such rehearsals are a wonderful social outlet as well as a tremendous aid to musical preparation.

Perhaps select one other member from your section. If possible, invite mostly those who do not sing your vocal part so you do not have anyone to lean on musically. However, it is always beneficial to schedule time with a few members of your section as well.

Your careful preparation will pay huge dividends musically, as you are able to contribute fully to the success of your chorus.

THE DRESS REHEARSAL

Before the scheduled performance (usually the night before), a dress rehearsal will take place to give the chorus an opportunity to sing the concert literature in the performance venue. The dress rehearsal does not require the singers to come dressed in concert attire unless the performance involves an opera chorus or special costumes for pop chorus productions.

At the dress rehearsal, stay focused and limit questions as much as possible. The conductor will instruct the chorus on how to walk on stage and off stage, which hand to carry the folder in if music is used, and when to raise the folder. He or she will also listen for balance, diction, and dynamics and will make suggestions to improve the performance experience.

If an orchestra is involved, the conductor will make suggestions to both groups during the dress rehearsal. Remain flexible and listen to the instructions from the conductor at all times. You will want to make notes in the score as a reminder of directions given during the dress rehearsal. In longer works, standing and sitting cues will be discussed. Write them in.

There is a saying among musicians that "a bad dress rehearsal means a good performance." A good performance should not be the goal. An organization should strive for a remarkable dress rehearsal and a breathtaking concert performance. Both the dress rehearsal and the performance should be a rewarding experience for all involved.

CHAPTER

SCORE MARKING FOR SINGERS

Many singers do not have a clear score-marking system, as we are never really taught how to mark a score to bring about all the musicality the conductor asks for in rehearsals. This chapter will suggest a general system of score marking to be used in the rehearsal process and to serve as a reminder in performance to bring about a higher level of music making. It is vitally important to mark the score appropriately and to follow your marks to the letter to accomplish musical consistency in an ensemble. Do not attempt to memorize your marks, as a visual reminder will serve you much better. Train yourself to obey the pencil marks each and every time. The more you reinforce great musicality through attention to the minute details of the score, the more you will grow musically over time. This process may take a little more time in the beginning stages, but the rewards will be great.

Purchase a copy of each piece you are performing for your personal library. You will be able to mark the score as desired and may use the markings again in future performances. However, keep in mind that the markings will need to be adjusted for another conductor, who may interpret the work differently, or to reflect changes in interpretation by your own conductor.

Please do not make illegal copies of music at any time. If you choose to make a copy of the music to be performed for study purposes, the copy *must* originate from a purchased copy, either by the singer or the choral organization. To learn more about music copyright and choral music, see Hinshaw Music's wonderful guide *Copyright and the Choral Musician* online at www.hinshawmusic.com/copyright.html.

GENERAL MARKINGS

1. Number each measure in the piece of music. If the first measure is not a complete measure, begin numbering in the first full measure as shown in figure 6.1.

Figure 6.1 Youll *While Joyful Springtime Lasteth*

2. Highlight your voice part if you are having trouble following the part, especially in larger works or double chorus music.

3. Often, conductors will give adjectives to describe the mood of a piece or other interpretive descriptions. Write these adjectives in the musical score to focus your memory at rehearsals and in the performance.

4. You may "lift" your entrance note from another voice part or a repeated note in your own part. Hear the note inside—called inner hearing—rather than humming

the note during the rest, however. In figure 6.2, the sopranos may lift their entrance note from the preceding alto note. Draw a line connecting the alto pitch to the soprano pitch. This type of marking also focuses the eyes and ears of the singer on a part other than his or her own. The singer may also take his or her note from a soloist or from the accompaniment.

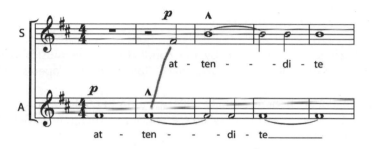

Figure 6.2 Vittoria *O vos omnes*

5. Place a small "x" above or below a note or series of missed notes or rhythms in a measure. As you work out the problem areas in the music in your private rehearsal, erase the mark. Ask for assistance from your section leader or conductor when needed. Perhaps there is just one note or rhythm that you are missing.

6. Write in any special accents, phrase markings, or dynamics given by the conductor in rehearsal.

7. Circle loud dynamic markings and draw a box around softer dynamics. As you study your music prior to rehearsal, you may wish to use colored pencils (blue for soft and red for loud) to indicate dynamic levels. The colors serve as a great visual reminder to the singer.

8. Enlarge crescendos and decrescendos in the score. Write in crescendos and decrescendos as a visual aid when *cresc.* and *decresc.* appear as text in the music rather than the symbols. As with the dynamic markings, a blue colored pencil may be used to trace a decrescendo and a red pencil used for crescendo.

9. If your chorus memorizes the music, write in a big "MEM" to remind you of sections that need extra work memory-wise.

10. Write in directives such as "watch" (some singers draw a pair of glasses in the score), "don't move," and "turn quietly."

TONE AND TEXT MARKINGS

1. Write descriptive words given by the conductor in the musical score. Some examples include "tall," "round," "lyric," "dark," "full," "rich," and "open space."

2. Use International Phonetic Alphabet (IPA) symbols to reinforce correct vowel and consonant sounds of a word or syllable, especially in foreign texts. Refer to the IPA chart in Resource A.

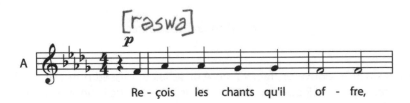

Figure 6.3 Fauré *Cantique de Jean Racine*

3. Place an ╱ over stressed syllables or notes and an ◡ over unstressed syllables or notes in the score.

Figure 6.4 Marenzio *Fiere silvestre*

4. Double underline a consonant that needs to be crisper or sharper. In the example in figure 6.5, the "m" sound in the word "lament" needs to be prolonged, and the "k" sound in the word "cry" needs to be very crisp. In the case of a prolonged humming consonant such as *m*, write in another *m* as a reminder to prolong the sound.

Figure 6.5 Jones *Lament My Soul*

5. Place a box around words where the vowel sound tends to spread in such words as "and," "have," "as," and "had." You may also write descriptives like "round" or "tall" in the score. In the excerpt in figure 6.6, the word "Lamb" will tend to spread. Place a box around the word to remind yourself to round out the sound each time.

Figure 6.6 Handel "Behold the Lamb of God" from *Messiah*

6. Write final consonants in the score for clear cut-offs. The final "p" of "sheep" in figure 6.7 must be pronounced sharply on the second beat. Write a "p" under the rest as a visual reminder.

Figure 6.7 Handel "All We Like Sheep Have Gone Astray" from *Messiah*

7. Use a forward slash as shown in figure 6.8 to avoid eliding consonant to vowel in the text.

Figure 6.8 Handel "For Unto Us a Child Is Born" from *Messiah*

8. When a text appears in two languages, some singers find it less confusing to the eye to cross out the language not used. Translations, for the most part, are poor in many choral editions on the market today. A word-by-word translation may be written above the soprano line or directly below the singer's voice part if room permits.

9. When asked to elide two consonants or a consonant to a vowel (e.g., in French), join the two letters together with a curved line (e.g., égal au)

INTONATION MARKINGS

1. Use an up arrow to indicate a higher pitch on a note and a down arrow to indicate a lower pitch on a note. In figure 6.9, the d-flat to the d-natural in the tenor line needs to be a higher interval, and the d-natural to the c-natural should feel lower in the voice.

Figure 6.9 Beethoven *Der glorreiche Augenblick*

2. One of the easiest mistakes to make in reading a piece for the first time is to miss a repeated note, especially if that repeated note is an enharmonic tone. An enharmonic tone sounds the same, but is spelled differently. In figure 6.10, the d-flat at the end of the second measure is enharmonic with the c-sharp in the next measure. Therefore, the pitch does not change at all. When you encounter repeated pitches or enharmonic tones in the score, circle the notes and write "SAME" so you do not try to change the pitch.

Figure 6.10 Verdi *Ave Maria*

3. Solfeggio is a wonderful intonation and music-reading tool. For those singers with experience in solfeggio, write the syllables in your voice part to reinforce better intonation. Although you may not need to use this technique for the entire work, use it in tricky spots to clarify the pitch. To determine the key of a piece, both with solfeggio and letter names, refer to Resource C: Key Signatures.

Figure 6.11 Bach *Jesu, meine Freude*

4. To differentiate between half and whole steps, especially in very chromatic passages, bracket the intervals as shown in figure 6.12. It is helpful to also write either "half" or "whole" above the bracket.

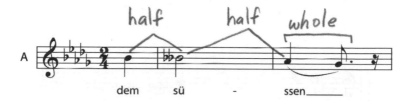

Figure 6.12 Brahms "Rote Abendwolken" from *Zigeunerlieder*

5. Write in an accidental when it is repeated in a bar. Accidentals are good for one measure of music unless cancelled by another accidental. The a-sharp in the second measure of the tenor line in figure 6.13 is good for the final note in the measure as well. However, since there was no sharp sign beside the note, it could easily be mistaken for an a-natural. Write in the sharp sign on "sus" of "Jesus" to clearly identify the true pitch.

Figure 6.13 Purcell *O God, The King of Glory*

TEMPO AND RHYTHM MARKINGS

1. To indicate a slowing of tempo, such as a final ritardando, mark the score with a horizontal wavy line (〜〜〜) or simply write "rit." in the score. Both options are used in figure 6.14. Use the one that makes the most sense to you.

Figure 6.14 Bach "O grosse Lieb" from *St. John Passion*

2. For phrases that tend to drag, especially in softer singing, use a forward arrow → to remind yourself to move the phrase ahead.

3. For phrases that tend to rush, especially very rhythmic phrases or during a crescendo, use a backward arrow ← to remind yourself to keep the tempo steady.

4. A forward arrow may also be used to remind the singer to hold a note for its full duration. This particular marking originates from the note, connecting it to the rest that follows in figure 6.15, reminding the sopranos not to shorten the final quarter note in each measure.

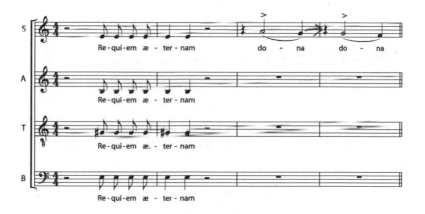

Figure 6.15 Verdi "Requiem aeternam" from *Messa di Requiem*

5. Number the beats in bars that contain complicated rhythms for rhythmic clarity. Notes in the second and third measures in figure 6.16 from Verdi's "Stabat Mater" occur on beats 1 and 3. To further clarify the rhythm, beats 2 and 4 may be written with smaller numbers.

Figure 6.16 Verdi "Stabat Mater" from *Quattro Pezzi Sacri*

6. Divide each beat into smaller units to clarify a syncopated (disturbance of the normal pulse) rhythm. In the 4/4 example in figure 6.17, using the Verdi "Stabat Mater" once again, the quarter notes are divided into eighth notes to clarify the syncopated rhythm in the soprano part.

Chri - sti si vi de-ret in tan - to sup - pli - ci - o?

Figure 6.17 Verdi "Stabat Mater" from *Quattro Pezzi Sacri*

7. Place a box around or enlarge meter signature changes in the musical score. In figure 6.18, the meter changes from 5 to 4. Write a big 5 and a big 4 in your score as a visual reference. If a change of meter happens over a page turn, write the meter change in the margin at the bottom of the previous page as a reminder.

Figure 6.18 Vittoria *Ave Maria*

PHRASE MARKINGS

1. Breath marks should always be placed in the score. It is not wise to rely on memory, for you will most likely find yourself breathing in incorrect spots that will break the flow of the phrase. When the breaths are marked in, you are training yourself to pace the breath and will begin to develop good breathing habits that will fuel the energy in every phrase you sing.

    A symbol like a large comma is used to mark breaths in the score. Some singers use a check mark. Whatever your system, just make sure it works for you.

Figure 6.19 Brahms *O schöne Nacht*

2. To indicate no breath in a phrase, use a broken line or write the words "no breath" in the score. In the Bach example in figure 6.20, your conductor may choose to carry the breath over after the fermata.

Figure 6.20 Bach *Jesu, meine Freude*

3. Imitation occurs when one part duplicates a melody previously sung in another part. Take, for instance, "Let Us Break Their Bonds Asunder" from *Messiah* in figure 6.21. The soprano part imitates the tenor part, and the alto part imitates the bass part. As an initial reminder on first study, you may want to connect the parts with a line just to remind yourself to listen to the imitation as it occurs from part to part.

Figure 6.21 Handel "Let Us Break Their Bonds Asunder" from *Messiah*

4. Whereas imitation is an exact duplication of the pitch, a sequence is the repetition of a pattern on a higher or lower pitch. These patterns allow the singer to learn several notes at once. Place a bracket around notes in a sequence and write the word "sequence" over it.

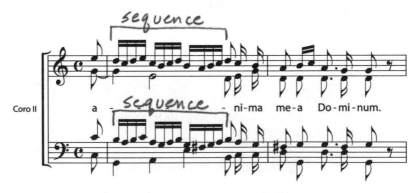

Figure 6.22 Pachelbel *Magnificat*

5. Use a plus sign (+) to mark the peak of a phrase in vocal music (see bass part in figure 6.23) or a crooked arrow to signify forward movement to the phrase peak (tenor line in figure 6.23). The peak of the phrase is the climax (tension) of the phrase. The energy of the vocal line moves the singer to this point in the music, which is then followed by relaxation or resolution.

Figure 6.23 Brahms *Der Abend*

6. Page turns can really get in the way of a consistent phrase. Very often, page turns occur in the worst possible places, especially during melismas and in very fast music. Extend the measure in the score to maintain the forward momentum of the phrase. The bass part has been extended in the example in figure 6.24.

Figure 6.24 Handel "Since By Man Came Death" from *Messiah*

7. First and second endings are usually placed over the soprano line. Mark them clearly in your part, and enlarge repeat signs to keep the eye focused on them in rehearsal and performance.

Figure 6.25 Weelkes *Young Cupid Hath Proclaimed*

Note

If you have creative score-marking ideas that you would like to share for a future edition of *The Choral Singer's Survival Guide*, please e-mail them to tthornton@vocalplanet.net.

CHAPTER

THE CHORAL PERFORMANCE

**"The greatest respect an artist can
pay to music is to give it life."**

Pablo Casals

The ultimate goal of the choral rehearsal is to prepare for the performance. After much work on the part of the singers, music staff, board of directors, parents, and volunteers, the performance affords the organization an opportunity to share the music with its beloved audience.

In addition to regular concert performances with your own chorus, opportunities to sing in regional choruses, all-state choruses, choral festivals, and on tour will provide you with valuable experience. The more you perform, the better you become at performing.

BECOME AN AMBASSADOR FOR YOUR CHORUS

As a member of the choral ensemble, especially a not-for-profit organization, more is required of you than merely a great voice and attendance at rehearsals. Each singer must become an ambassador for his or her choral group, spreading the word about upcoming concerts and special events to friends, family, and acquaintances who are interested in the arts. Send e-mail invitations and make personal phone calls to invite these people.

Spending just a few hours promoting your choral concert can have a dramatic impact on ticket sales for the concert or season.

The chorus marketing committee or department will most likely produce materials such as concert flyers or postcards announcing the concert. Distribute the flyers and postcards in neighborhood music stores and in the windows of other appropriate shops. Having family and friends at concerts is wonderful, but the organization will need to attract additional audience members to maintain financial security.

Most choruses have a website these days, so make sure this information is placed on all materials including e-mails you send out. Although many choruses check out tickets to their members, tickets may also be purchased through the chorus website or through ticketing agencies.

If you are not a great salesperson or do not feel comfortable selling, team up with a fellow chorus member who is. It would be very unfortunate to walk out on stage to find only half the concert venue filled. Yet imagine how wonderful it will feel as you walk out on the stage to find a packed house or even a sold-out concert. Make sure to do your part.

THE CARE AND PRESERVATION OF THE VOICE

As a singer, you have worked very hard over a period of weeks to prepare for the performance. It would be a pity to become ill right before the concert. Concert week may include additional rehearsals and certainly a dress rehearsal. This added stress could cause the immune system to weaken, making the body susceptible to illness. Cramming to learn the music at the last minute will also create a great deal of unnecessary stress in the body and, therefore, in the voice.

Below are some suggestions for maintaining good vocal health.

1. Strive for good general physical and mental health at all times through exercise, meditation, and proper diet.
2. Get plenty of rest. If the body is tired, the voice is tired.
3. Along with a proper diet, a daily multivitamin, extra Vitamin C, or zinc may help the singer to remain healthy. However, always consult a physician before adding these supplements.
4. Always warm up the voice.
5. Always speak and sing with proper alignment and breath support.
6. Avoid loud talking, screaming, and "wheezing" or stressed laughter.
7. Avoid speaking in loud environments.
8. Those who must use their voices for a extended period of time each day, especially teachers, should try to develop as many nonverbal ways of communicating as possible. The Voice Academy online at www.voiceacademy.org has many helpful suggestions. A free registration is required, but teachers and public speakers will learn a variety of ways to preserve the voice.
9. Constant throat clearing irritates the vocal cords. Swallow or take a sip of water in lieu of clearing the throat.
10. Speak at a comfortable pitch range. Do not speak too high or too low, as this will cause wear and tear on the voice. If you find that your voice becomes tired, scratchy, or irritated easily from speaking, consult with a voice professional immediately.
11. Maintain hydration by drinking 8 to 10 glasses of water each day. Those with larger bodies may need more. Remember, the vocal cords are one of the last organs to receive the benefits of water. Drinks made with water such as tea or coffee do not count toward the daily recommended amount.
12. Diuretics such as caffeine, alcohol, and artificially flavored beverages remove moisture from the body, and therefore the voice. Avoid them as much as possible before a concert performance.
13. Medications such as antihistamines, allergy pills, and birth control pills may cause dryness in the throat. An increased intake of water will be necessary if you are prescribed such medications.
14. As for smoking anything, just don't do it. Also avoid second-hand smoke as much as possible. Not only does smoking rob the vocal cords of much-needed moisture, continued smoking damages the lungs, thus decreasing the breath capacity and range of the singer.
15. Food and drinks high in acids or sugar such as colas and citrus or tomato products should be avoided before singing. Also avoid dairy products such as milk, cheese,

ice cream, or yogurt, which may cause the production of too much phlegm for comfortable singing.

16. Spicy and salty foods in large amounts may cause dryness of the throat.
17. Chewing gum before a rehearsal or performance is not recommended. For the gum to remain moist—notice, it comes dry in the wrapper—it uses saliva, which reduces the moisture level inside the mouth.
18. Some singers are negatively affected by air conditioning, heating, mold, and perfumes. Avoid them as much as possible prior to the performance.
19. Reduce the general usage of the voice before a concert. Speak less and enjoy periods of quiet reflection. Much of your music study does not require singing. Go through the music mentally.
20. Do not try to sing over a cold, especially when a sore throat is involved. Lozenges or throat sprays should not be used to numb the throat in order to sing. If the throat is sore, do not sing or speak at all. Whispering does not save or rest the voice. In fact, it is probably the worst thing you can do when experiencing a sore throat. Rest the voice completely.

It is up to you, sometimes with the help of a doctor or voice professional, to assess your own challenges and possible remedies to prevent sickness before the performance. Make sure to take the proper steps to the best of your ability, with common sense as your guide, to ensure a vocally healthy, enriching concert experience.

CONCERT ETIQUETTE

You should instruct family members and friends on proper concert etiquette prior to the concert. Remember, the audience is paying good money to enjoy the concert and the chorus has worked diligently for many weeks or months toward the performance. The performance will most likely be recorded, and it would be a shame for a noisy audience member or a misbehaving child to disrupt the concert and potentially compromise the quality of the recording.

Children should have the opportunity to hear great live music. However, they are often too young to sit through a two-hour choral concert. Parents should use their best judgment when bringing a small child to a concert. In any event, sitting near an exit is a great idea in case the child becomes restless. Some choruses offer a family concert or children's concert as part of the subscription series.

Below are some basic rules of concert etiquette to pass on to friends and family before the concert.

1. Dress appropriately for the concert. Although an outside concert may be a casual outing, a concert in a more prestigious venue warrants sharper dress.
2. Arrive at least 30 minutes before the beginning of the concert to find parking, purchase tickets, locate your seat, and review the concert program. In the case of a late arrival, ushers usually seat between pieces or sets, so do not get upset with the usher if you are late. If there is balcony seating, it may be possible to go directly into the concert, however.
3. Videotaping, flash photography, and audio recording are not allowed in many concert venues. Please respect these requests, as they are most often policy set forth by the management of the performance venue. Ignoring policies such as this may put the group at risk of losing the opportunity to perform in the venue. In addition, these activities are distracting not only to those onstage but to audience members as well.
4. Cell phones, pagers, and alarms on watches should always be turned off before the concert begins. There is no excuse for a cell phone to ring during a concert.
5. They are not to scream out your name when you arrive on stage or when you leave the stage area. Believe it or not, this happens at choral concerts. The response to this unwelcome behavior is usually displeasure on the part of the conductor and embarrassment on the part of the chorus member.
6. Tell friends and family not to wave at you from the audience. Even if they do, you cannot wave back at them.
7. It is absolutely fine to clap loudly as the chorus arrives on stage. There is nothing like a great reception from the audience at the beginning of the concert.
8. Depending on the chosen program, the audience may clap after each piece or after a set is completed. If an audience member is unsure, just wait until everyone else starts clapping. The most experienced audience members will know when to clap and when not. At times, an instruction to refrain from clapping may be included inside the concert program.
9. Talking or whispering during the concert disturbs those around you. Listen and enjoy, don't talk.
10. If an audience member has a coughing episode during the concert, he or she should try to leave the performance as quickly and quietly as possible. Sitting near an exit if you are recovering from a cold is the best plan. However, do not unwrap lozenges during the concert, as this noise will distract the chorus and those seated nearby.

11. There will usually be a 10- to 15-minute intermission in the middle of the performance. A bell may be sounded or lights dimmed to signal the beginning of the second half.
12. A standing ovation at the end of the concert is always welcome along with a "Bravo!" to show appreciation for the incredible work that has gone into preparing the concert.

CONCERT PREPARATION

Remember to have your concert attire cleaned a few days before the performance. Plan to pick up your items from the cleaners on the day before the concert to prevent added stress before you sing.

During the day of the concert, relax as much as possible. However, if you are feeling a bit nervous, meditate or go shopping or out to a movie to relax. Visualization also calms the mind and focuses the intention of the singer on a great performance experience. Envision yourself walking onto the stage with complete confidence, performing a marvelous concert, singing every note of every piece beautifully and musically, and the thunderous applause from the audience at the completion of the concert.

Drink plenty of water throughout the day to stay hydrated. Review the suggestions in the section "Care and Preservation of the Voice."

Taking a nap during the day is fine as long as you do not feel sluggish for the concert. It is important to feel refreshed and energetic to make great music in the performance. A hot shower or bath will revive you after a nap.

Do not overeat before the concert. However, do have a light meal to provide the energy needed for the concert. Singers who do not eat before a concert tend to sing under the pitch due to a lack of energy.

Look your very best for the concert. Make sure you are well groomed. Women and men with long hair should pull the hair back so that the audience can see the face and eyes clearly. Do not wear large jewelry that distracts from the face. As some singers are very sensitive to perfumes, colognes, or hairspray, avoid wearing them. However, do use unscented deodorant.

Remember to take the music with you to the performance. Gentlemen, check to make sure you have your tie, cummerbund, and studs if wearing a tux.

Plan for traffic, and arrive at the concert venue early. As in the audition, you do not want the stress of being late to affect the performance. Arrive early, warm up the voice, and make some final mental notes before the chorus warm-up on stage.

The chorus will most likely meet at the venue early to warm up and sing through pieces prior to the start of the concert. The conductor will give final reminders about interpretation, sound, articulation, and so on. In most instances, the conductor will start the pieces and briefly rehearse selected sections of the work. Stay focused during this time and listen carefully.

Visit the restroom before the concert call time. A room will usually be designated to house purses, coats, and other valuables during the performance. Make sure to place your belongings in the room before the concert begins.

"AND THE CROWD GOES WILD..."

If this is your first choral performance or first performance in a while, you may feel a bit nervous. However, focus on the excitement of the performance and the impact the music will have on the performers and the audience. Before you enter the stage area, remember that the performance has the power to change lives—not only the singers' but also those listening. Vocal music has so many positive effects on the body, mind, and spirit. It benefits us in ways that we do not fully understand. Put your heart and soul into the performance, and the nervousness will subside.

The performance may bring about any number of emotions in the singers and the audience—laughter, tears, and joy. Vocal music has such a profound effect on the audience because the musical line contains text. It is the words coupled with a beautiful sound and understanding of the music that reaches directly into the hearts of those listening.

As you enter the stage area, smile. Show the audience that you are proud to be a member of the chorus and happy to be singing in the concert performance. Engage the audience before the first note of the piece is sung. An initial pleasant expression is very inviting to the audience. It says, "Welcome and thank you for joining us this evening. You are in for a real treat." An unpleasant expression will turn the audience off immediately. If the chorus is to be seated onstage, watch for the cue to sit from the designated person.

The conductor and accompanist will usually enter after the chorus. If an orchestra is involved, the concertmaster will enter the stage area first to tune the orchestra. Upon entering, the conductor will often have the orchestra stand and, if the chorus is seated, they will be asked to stand as well. The standing and sitting cues will have been worked out in the dress rehearsal.

If instrumentalists are not used and the chorus is not seated, the conductor will merely give a gesture to raise the folders to begin the concert. Watch the conductor at all times.

Make sure to keep your body alignment in check during the concert. Keep the knees flexible. Locking the knees can cause fainting. However, avoid excessive movements, as they will be distracting to the other singers and the audience. Even the smallest movement on stage looks much larger to the audience. Keep the hands away from your hair and face while singing.

Proper alignment and an open space when breathing will ensure a deep-seated, yet quiet breath. Remember to keep the body open throughout the act of singing. A loud breath, especially during very soft or intimate moments, will spoil the mood of the music.

Do not overdo facial expressions, but show an expression that reflects the mood of the music. The singer should literally become the music. A singer who feels the need to "perform" will stick out from the audience's viewpoint. Usually, such a singer just wants attention. However, the focus should remain on the performance of the group rather than the individual singer.

Turn pages as quietly as possible, especially in very soft passages. For a singer who holds the music in the right hand, use the thumb and index or third finger (whichever is more comfortable) of the left hand to grasp the bottom right edge of the page for a quiet turn. For a singer who holds the music in the left hand, use the thumb and index or third finger of the right hand to turn the page. However, do not wait until you reach the bottom of the page to prepare this action. Once the singer reaches the top of the next page, this process should begin immediately to ensure a quiet and quick page turn. Paperclip a series of pages or a movement in which you do not sing.

If the concert involves a soloist, do not follow the music along with the soloist. Turn to the next entrance of the chorus, yet keep your attention focused on the conductor. Remain a part of the music even when you are not singing.

Mistakes happen. However, keep going and do not call attention to them. Stay focused and get back on track with the music immediately. Do not allow one mistake to destroy an entire page or piece of music.

Both the chorus and the orchestra will need the conductor when forces are combined in a concert. Choruses tend to rely heavily on the conductor. However, the conductor will be unable to focus exclusively on the chorus. Follow the score markings to a tee. It is the responsibility of the singer to bring life to everything in the musical score, whether or not the conductor gives a cutoff or entrance.

An intermission of about 10 to 15 minutes will normally take place during the concert. Smaller choruses will usually leave the stage. Be mindful of cues given by the conductor to walk on or off stage, especially if you are leading the group's entrance or exit.

Large symphonic choruses may remain on stage during the intermission. Those who need to use the restroom or have a drink of water are usually permitted to leave the stage area to do so, however. Again, this information will be communicated to the singers at the dress rehearsal.

Whenever the audience applauds, accept the applause. Smile and let audience members know that you appreciate their support and enthusiasm. It is usually not preferred that singers clap at the conclusion of the concert. At the end of the concert, the chorus will take a bow. If the audience continues to applaud loudly, an encore may be performed unless the concert literature is a major work. Watch the conductor carefully so that you bow with everyone else. Leave the stage area with a smile for a job well done.

AFTERGLOW

Following the concert and before you greet your adoring fans, the music should be returned if it is borrowed from the chorus. An announcement to this effect will be made in the final rehearsals. Some choruses place a box backstage for music return. Please do your part to make the job of the chorus librarian easier. It is a thankless, yet essential job that involves a lot of work.

Refrain from discussing mistakes that may have happened during the concert to keep the experience positive for everyone involved.

Some choruses have a reception following the concert. If not, friends and family will normally greet the performers in the lobby of the performance venue. Enthusiastic fans will certainly provide input and talk about favorite pieces, and you may have a stranger come up to you to inquire about auditions for the group. Great performances are the best way to recruit singers into a choral organization. There may have been a young child or young adult in the audience who had never heard music in a concert setting before. Your choral concert may have been so inspiring as to call this young person to pursue music as a career.

The singers will invariably hear stories of how a certain piece of music moved an audience member and perhaps changed his or her life. Moments such as these make all of the effort put forth in rehearsals, both private and group, worth every second.

Celebrate your personal achievements during the concert preparation and performance and the success of the choral ensemble. You have certainly earned it.

It has been a great pleasure to guide you on your journey to locate, prepare, audition for, and perform in a chorus. Following this chapter is a valuable resource section to help you further increase your musical knowledge. May the information in this book serve you and the choral arts for many years to come. Keep singing!

❧ Resources ❧

A CRASH COURSE IN SINGERS' DICTION

Perhaps part of your reason for joining an ensemble is to communicate a powerful message through music. Great diction is one of the hallmarks of a great chorus. Diction is the combination of pronunciation, enunciation, and articulation in singing. *Pronunciation* is the manner in which a singer produces a word with regard to both sound color and syllable stress. *Enunciation*, to bring forth or make known, refers to the level of intelligibility regarding the fullness and clarity of the sound. *Articulation* refers to the action of the speech organs in the formation of vowels, consonants, syllables, and words. To a singer or instrumentalist, articulation also refers to the execution of interpretive elements such as accents, legato, marcato, and staccato.

Crisp, clean diction affects not only textual understanding but also intonation, rhythm, and tone color. If the singers in a chorus do not sing the same vowel sound, intonation is flawed. When singers produce lazy consonants and move slowly to the vowel, rhythm is unstable. In both instances, tone quality suffers. As group singers, we must strive for a uniform sound within the choral ensemble at all times. In short, every member of the chorus must care about every sound every second. It is that important.

BASIC RULES OF DICTION

Although each language is unique, they all share common principles. A mastery of the following simple principles will improve the clarity of ensemble (and solo) diction immediately. As each individual choral singer in an ensemble begins to transfer and use these basic rules on a consistent basis throughout the choral repertoire, the sound of both the individual singer and the choral ensemble will become more unified and engaging.

1. Prolong the vowel sound of every word or syllable for as long as possible.
2. Begin the vowel sound on the beat. This means that a consonant or consonant pair must begin slightly ahead of the beat. Every sound is time specific.

3. When a diphthong (two vowel sounds in succession) appears in a word, hold the first vowel sound for as long as possible before releasing it to the second vowel.
4. Make consonants very crisp and energetic, springing directly to the vowel. Consonants may be softened slightly depending on the language.
5. Phonate every sound in every syllable, especially consonants appearing in the middle of a word and final humming consonants.
6. Remember that every language has a natural word stress that gives color and meaning to the word. No two adjacent syllables are stressed alike. However, "weaker" syllables link the sound to the next strong syllable, creating forward motion in a phrase.
7. Do not elide a final consonant at the end of one word to a vowel or vowel sound at the beginning of a new word. There must be a clean beginning to the new word. The exceptions to this rule are *liaison* in French and *elision* in French and Italian.
8. As a general rule, pronounce the neutral vowel [ə] between adjacent consonants either in the middle of a word or when a consonant appears at the end of a word moving into another consonant of a new word. In some cases, the conductor may choose to elide two consonants.
9. When moving from a vowel sound of one word into a vowel sound (same or different) of a new word, give a slight crescendo on the first vowel and lean into the second vowel sound for a smooth, legato line. This will prevent an unnecessary glottal attack.

A DICTION PRIMER

Great diction does not happen by accident. As singers, we have a tremendous responsibility to the text we are performing and to communicating that text effectively to our audience. Although many texts, especially those of the Catholic Mass, are familiar to many listeners, a great many texts are not. Without intelligible diction, we offer the audience only half an experience.

Choruses display the same diction habits as a soloist displays but due to the number of singers in an ensemble, the effects of poor habits (e.g., no final consonants, stressed syllables that should not be stressed) is multiplied. Rehearsal at home by every singer and a strong commitment to lucid diction by the conductor will pave the way to a polished performance and extraordinary musical experience for both the performer and the audience.

Although it is not within the scope of this book to offer an in-depth study of diction for singing, the pages that follow will present the choral singer with the basic elements of English, Latin, Italian, German, and French in a very user-friendly format. This information will provide the singer with simple, yet powerful, solutions to the most common errors in diction.

The International Phonetic Alphabet (IPA)

Developed by British and French phoneticians, the International Phonetic Alphabet (IPA) was established in Paris in 1896 as a model to encourage uniformity in speaking and singing. The alphabet has gone through a number of revisions, with the last one occurring in 1996.

A command of the sounds present in the IPA will lead the singer toward an appropriate pronunciation in each of the languages covered in this book.

For the convenience of the reader, both the IPA and a nonphonetic sound sample for each example in Latin and Italian are included here. However, French and German are not easily written out nonphonetically, as the nonphonetic spelling does not capture the sound of the word. For those languages, only IPA is used so that the singer clearly understands the correct sound of the word.

The IPA Chart of Symbols that follows is broken down into four parts: the IPA symbol, an example to approximate the sound of the symbol, the character of each consonant and vowel, and the languages that use the sound.

The IPA Symbol and Example

Symbols may be used singularly or in conjunction with other symbols to spell out a complete word, which may be longer than the original word in IPA, for example, [ɛ] = *eh*; [kristɛ] = krEE-steh.

Although many singers write out the sound of a word nonphonetically in their scores, take the time to familiarize yourself with IPA as a rehearsal tool and for a more precise guide to polished pronunciation. The IPA is a consistent, visual representation of a single sound or complete word, whereas writing out words as they sound to you is not. In addition, other singers, teachers, and vocal coaches will be able to read and make sense out of your markings.

To approximate the sound of each symbol, the chart includes either a familiar example or foreign example with further directions for pronunciation when an English equivalent is not available. For instance, to correctly pronounce [œ], the singer will sing an open e [ɛ] eh on the inside with the tip of the tongue forward (behind the lower teeth) through the round-lip position of open o [ɔ] aw. In other words, sing an [ɛ] eh vowel through the round-lip position of [ɔ] aw.

Character

The lines in the character column of the chart identify several key characteristics of each sound. In the case of a vowel sound, the character line specifies if the vowel is closed (long), open (short), nasal, neutral, or a diphthong. In the case of consonants, the consonants are grouped into categories indicating their similar characteristics and method of production in singing diction. A brief description of the articulators needed (lips, tongue, etc.) for the production of the sound is also included as an aid to correct pronunciation. In addition, consonants are listed as either voiced (there is a vibration of the vocal instrument) or unvoiced (there is not a vibration of the vocal instrument). All vowels are voiced and several consonants are voiced. Voiced consonants carry pitch whereas unvoiced consonants do not. Therefore, it is paramount for the singer to know the difference between the two to avoid pitch distortion. The singer must begin and end voiced consonants in the center of the pitch the consonant appears on.

If you are thinking to yourself one day, "Hey! I wonder if [f] is voiced or unvoiced," try this very simple test:

Place your thumb and index finger on each side of the Adam's apple. Sound an [f] as in the word *forte*. You will notice that there is no vibration of the vocal instrument. Therefore [f] is an unvoiced consonant. Now, sound the letter [v] as in *voice*. You will notice that there is a vibration of the vocal instrument, indicating that [v] is a voiced consonant.

Character Definitions

affricate The consonant combination of a stop-plosive and a fricative forming a single sound.

bilabial A sound created with both lips.

closed (long) vowel A vowel of long duration (generally twice as long) as an open (short) vowel. In vocal terms, "closed" simply means less space in the front of the mouth. However, there is still a feeling of "yawn" in the back.

continuant A sound that may be continued as long as the breath supply permits. All consonants except for stop-plosives are continuants.

diphthong Two vowel sounds in the same syllable. The primary vowel sound is held for as long as possible before releasing it to the second vowel sound. The second vowel is sounded very quickly as a fading vowel before the next sound.

fricative A sound produced when two articulators (e.g., upper teeth and lower lip) close together. Air flowing through the narrow passage creates the sound of "friction."

glide A vowel-like sound (often written as a consonant) that "glides" very quickly into an oncoming vowel; often called semiconsonant or semivowel.

lateral A sound produced when the tip of the tongue makes contact with the upper teeth or gum as air escapes through one or both sides of the tongue.

nasal (humming) consonant A humming sound produced when air is allowed to escape through the nose, as the oral passageway is blocked by either the lips or tongue.

nasal vowel An open sound produced when air is allowed to escape through the nose and mouth simultaneously.

neutral vowel An unstressed or unaccented sound, generally referred to as the schwa [ə].

open (short) vowel A vowel that is normally of shorter duration than the closed (long) vowel sound. However, the defining characteristic of the open (short) vowel is that the tongue is positioned as far as possible from the roof of the mouth.

palatal consonant A consonant that is articulated with the middle or back part of the tongue raised against the hard palate (the middle part of the roof of the mouth).

semivowel (semiconsonant) A consonant acting as a vowel sound within a word.

stop-plosive A sound produced by obstructing airflow with the lips or tongue.

IPA Chart of Symbols

Note: E = English, L = Latin, I = Italian, G = German, F = French

IPA Symbol	Example	Character	Languages
a	f<u>a</u>ther	Closed (long) vowel	E, L, I, G, F
ɒ	h<u>o</u>t	Open (short) vowel	E, G, F
ã	d<u>a</u>ns pond, without pronouncing *nd*	Open (short) nasal vowel	F
æ	c<u>a</u>t	Open (short) vowel	E
ai	m<u>ai</u>	Diphthong	L, I
aɪ	m<u>ei</u>n (*ah ih*)	Diphthong	E, G
au	l<u>au</u>date	Diphthong	L, I
aʊ	n<u>ow</u>	Diphthong	E, G
b	<u>b</u>ond	Voiced bilabial stop-plosive	E, L, I, G, F
ç	<u>h</u>uman	Unvoiced fricative	G
d	<u>d</u>ay	Voiced tongue-tip/gum ridge stop-plosive	E, L, I, G, F
dʒ	e<u>dge</u>	Voiced tongue-tip/gum ridge affricate	E, L, I
dz	bi<u>ds</u>	Voiced tongue-tip/gum ridge affricate	E, L, I
e	ch<u>a</u>otic	Closed (long) vowel	E, I, G, F

IPA Symbol	Example	Character	Languages
ɛ	s<u>e</u>t	Open (short) vowel	E, L, I, G, F
ə	<u>a</u>bout	Open (short) neutral vowel	E, G, F
ʌ	l<u>o</u>ve (*uh*)	Neutral vowel, the stressed equivalent of [ə]	E
ɛi	D<u>ei</u>	Diphthong	L, I
ɛɪ	m<u>ay</u>	Diphthong	E
ɛ̃	vi<u>en</u>s b<u>en</u>t, without pronouncing *nt*	Open (short) nasal vowel	F
f	<u>f</u>orte	Unvoiced lip/teeth fricative	E, L, I, G, F
g	<u>g</u>reen	Voiced velar stop-plosive	E, L, I, G, F
h	<u>h</u>arp	Unvoiced fricative	E, G
i	s<u>ee</u>	Closed (long) vowel	E, L, I, G, F
ɪ	p<u>i</u>t	Open (short) vowel	E, G
ɜ	bi<u>r</u>d	Open (short) vowel	E
j	<u>y</u>es	Voiced tongue/palatal semivowel glide	E, L, I, G, F
k	<u>k</u>ing	Unvoiced tongue/velar stop-plosive	E, L, I, G, F
l	<u>l</u>ine	Voiced tongue- tip/gum ridge lateral	E, L, I, G, F

(Continued)

IPA Symbol	Example	Character	Languages
ʎ	"lyee": A <u>single</u> movement of the front of the tongue against the front of the hard palate	Voiced lateral palatal	I
lj	mil<u>li</u>on: Two distinct movements of the tongue	Voiced tongue-tip /gum ridge lateral glide	E
m	<u>m</u>ezzo	Voiced bilabial/nasal/ humming consonant	E, L, I, G, F
n	<u>n</u>otation	Voiced tongue-tip /gum ridge /nasal/ humming consonant	E, L, I, G, F
ŋ	si<u>ng</u>	Voiced tongue /velar/nasal/ humming consonant	E, I, G
ɲ	opi<u>ni</u>on	Voiced tongue/gum ridge/ nasal/humming consonant	E, L, I, F
o	<u>o</u>bey	Closed (long) vowel	E, I, G, F
ɔ	f<u>ou</u>ght (*aw* with rounded lips)	Open (short) vowel	E, L, I, G, F
ø	tr<u>ö</u>sten (Ger.) Closed *e* [e] on the inside through a closed *o* [o] lip position	Closed (long) mixed vowel	G, F

IPA Symbol	Example	Character	Languages
õ	bon haunt, without pronouncing *nt*	Open (short) nasal vowel	F
œ	plötzlich (Ger.) Open *e* [ɛ] on the inside through an open *o* [ɔ] lip position	Open (short) mixed vowel	G, F
œ̃	un hunt, without pronouncing *nt*	Open (short) mixed vowel	F
ɔɪ	boy	Diphthong	E
ɔʊ	show	Diphthong	E, G
ɔø	Freude	Diphthong	G
p	piano	Unvoiced bilabial stop-plosive	E, L, I, G, F
ɹ	red	Voiced continuant and semi-vowel glide	E
ɾ	rosa flipped or rolled	Voiced continuant and semi-vowel glide	L, I, G, F (also British English)
s	sound	Unvoiced tongue/gum ridge fricative	E, L, I, G, F
ʃ	shine	Unvoiced tongue/palate fricative	E, L, I, G, F

(Continued)

IPA Symbol	Example	Character	Languages
t	<u>t</u>enor	Unvoiced tongue-tip/gum ridge stop-plosive	E, L, I, G, F
tʃ	pit<u>ch</u>	Unvoiced tongue-tip/gum ridge/palate affricate	E, L, I, F
ð	<u>th</u>y	Voiced tongue/teeth fricative	E
θ	ear<u>th</u>	Unvoiced tongue/teeth fricative	E
u	m<u>oo</u>n	Closed (long) vowel	E, L, I, G, F
ʊ	joyf<u>u</u>l	Open (short) vowel	E, G
v	<u>v</u>oice	Voiced lip/teeth fricative	E, L, I, G, F
w	<u>w</u>ind	Voiced bilabial semivowel glide	E, L, I, F
hw or ʍ	<u>wh</u>en	Unvoiced bilabial fricative/ semivowel glide	E
x	Ba<u>ch</u> The back of the tongue lifts toward the soft palate without contact	Unvoiced velar fricative	G
y	d<u>u</u> (Fr.) Closed *i* [i] on the inside through a closed *u* [u] lip position	Closed (long) mixed vowel	G, F

IPA Symbol	Example	Character	Languages
Y	würdig Open *i* [ɪ] on the inside through an open *u* [ʊ] lip position	Open (short) mixed vowel	G
z	mu_s_ic	Voiced tongue-tip/gum ridge fricative	E, L, I, G, F
ʒ	plea_s_ure	Voiced tongue blade/gum ridge fricative	E, F

ENGLISH DICTION

Whereas *L'Académie Française* exercises authority over the French language and similar bodies exist to preside over the Italian and German languages, there is no organization to oversee the correct usage or pronunciation of the English language. Correct English pronunciation for singers has been left in the hands of the many fine voice teachers, diction teachers, conductors, and coaches who probably found most of the answers to their own questions in either Madeleine Marshall's *The Singer's Manual of English Diction* or a wonderful book by Dorothy Uris titled *To Sing in English*.

English is often perceived to be a harsh-sounding language including naturally impure vowels that must contain a foreign substitute to make them beautiful. However when properly sung, English is a beautiful language full of resonance, stress, and release and tone colors, which can be very legato when combined with an even flow of breath, consonant clarity, and a unified vowel sound.

English Vowel Sounds

The spellings below represent some of the most common in the English language.

Spelling	Pronunciation	Example
a	[a] *ah* (long)	f<u>a</u>ther
	[e]	est<u>a</u>te
	[æ] (with very round lips to avoid a strident sound)	c<u>a</u>t
a, au, ou	[ɔ] *aw*	f<u>a</u>ll, <u>au</u>tumn <u>ou</u>ght
a, ai, au, e, io, ou	[ə] (see "Neutral Vowels" below)	mot<u>io</u>n, joy<u>ou</u>s <u>a</u>bout, fount<u>ai</u>n
e, ea	[ɛ] *eh*	s<u>e</u>t, pl<u>ea</u>sure
e, ee, ea, ei, eo, ie	[i] *ee*	m<u>e</u>, s<u>ee</u>, t<u>ea</u>cher
ear, ir, or, ur	[ɜ] (see "How to Handle the American *R*")	l<u>ear</u>n, b<u>ir</u>d w<u>or</u>d, t<u>ur</u>n
i, e, o, ui	[ɪ] *ih*	p<u>i</u>t, pr<u>e</u>tty w<u>o</u>men, b<u>ui</u>ld
o	[o] *oh* [ɒ] *ah* (short)	b<u>oa</u>t h<u>o</u>t
oo	[u] *oo* [ʊ]	m<u>oo</u>n l<u>oo</u>k
o, oo, ou, u	[ʌ] (see "Neutral Vowels" below)	d<u>ou</u>ble, l<u>u</u>ck l<u>o</u>ve, fl<u>oo</u>d

Neutral Vowel Sounds in English

The neutral vowel sounds of unstressed [ə] as in the word _about_ and its stressed counterpart, [ʌ], as in the word _love_, are very usable and appropriate sounds in the English language. One often hears exaggerated stress on final syllables, creating _angel_ [ɛndʒɛl] instead of _angel_ [ɛndʒəl]. This mispronunciation of the English language has become quite common with choral groups around the country. Neutral vowels play a vital role in the word stress in English, providing rhythmic contrasts within word rhythms and driving the melodic line forward through legato linkage to stronger syllables.

Diphthongs in English

The five most common diphthongs in English are [aɪ] as in the word _night_, [aʊ] _house_, [ɛɪ] _say_, [ɔɪ] _boy_, and [oʊ] as in _show_. Remember to hold the first vowel sound for as long as possible before releasing it to the second, or fading, vowel.

Glides

When a _u_ or _ew_ follows _d, n, l, s, t,_ or _th_ or when _r, y, w,_ or _wh_ (in several words) begins a word, a glide is created. In this case, the reverse of the diphthong rule occurs and the first vowel sound "glides" quickly to the second vowel sound, which is held. Two of the most common examples are the words _new_ and _dew_. Without the glide sound, the words would be _noo_ and _doo_. Other examples include _yes, red, wind,_ and _what_.

Consonants in Sung English

Consonants are grouped below as voiced or unvoiced and by the articulators involved in the production of the consonant. This information remains consistent for all the languages covered in _The Choral Singer's Survival Guide_. However, some of the consonants will be softened slightly depending on the language involved.

Consonants appearing across from one another on the chart are "partner" consonants or voiced and unvoiced counterparts. One of the consonants has tone, and the other is produced with air. However, both are produced by the same physical mechanism (e.g., both lips, tongue against gum ridge). Since these partner consonants are produced by the same physical mechanism, it is vitally important for the singer to distinguish clearly between the two sounds. One often hears the word _may_ instead of _make_ or _win_ instead of _when_, for instance, which can change the entire meaning of the text. To avoid this confusion, pronounce consonants with great intensity so that each word is crystal clear to the listener.

Production	Voiced	Unvoiced
Produced with both lips	[b] <u>b</u>aritone (stop-plosive) [m] <u>m</u>usic (nasal/humming) [w] <u>w</u>ind (semivowel glide)	[p] <u>p</u>iano (stop-plosive) [hw] or [ʍ] <u>wh</u>en (fricative/semivowel glide)
Produced with upper teeth and lower lip	[v] <u>V</u>erdi (fricative)	[f] <u>f</u>alsetto (fricative)
Produced with tongue pressed against the upper teeth	[ð] <u>th</u>y (fricative)	[θ] <u>th</u>eme (fricative)
Produced with the tip of the tongue on the gum ridge behind the upper teeth	[d] <u>d</u>rink (stop-plosive) [l] <u>l</u>ine (lateral) [n] <u>n</u>ote (nasal/humming) [dʒ] le<u>dg</u>er (affricate)	[t] <u>t</u>enor (stop-plosive) [tʃ] pit<u>ch</u> (affricate)
Produced with the tip of the tongue against the gum ridge	[ɹ] <u>r</u>hythm (continuant and semivowel glide) [z] <u>z</u>ero (fricative) [ʒ] mea<u>s</u>ure (fricative)	 [s] <u>s</u>ound (fricative) [ʃ] <u>sh</u>ine (fricative)
Produced with the middle of the tongue on the hard palate	[g] <u>g</u>reen (stop-plosive) [ŋ] si<u>ng</u> (nasal/humming) [j] <u>y</u>es (palatal semivowel glide)	[k] <u>k</u>ey (stop-plosive)
Produced with a breath shape	[h] <u>h</u>eart (fricative)	

Syllable Division

To maintain a legato sound in English, one must often alter the structure of syllables in the printed music score to maintain the integrity of the vowel sound. A consonant appearing at the end of a syllable should be sung at the beginning of the next syllable. If a double consonant appears within a word, sing only the second letter as illustrated below.

Written	Sung
ris-en	ri-sen
spok-en	spo-ken
Hal-le-lu-jah!	Ha-le-lu-jah!

How to Handle the American *R*

The American *r* [ɹ] is one of the most difficult sounds in the English language, as singers tend to lean on the sound making it sometimes unpleasant to the ear. However, with a clear understanding of a few basic rules, the choral singer will be able to produce an appropriate sound that energizes the word or syllable.

1. Always sing an *r* before a vowel if the vowel sound is not silent (*e.g., spirit*). The American *r* is articulated in the front of the mouth using the tip of the tongue against the gum ridge. The singer should have the feeling of "springing" to the vowel sound that follows. *R*'s may be flipped [ɾ] depending on the style of the music performed.
2. The neutral vowel [ə] is used for all words with two or more syllables ending in *r*: *lo-ver; Fa-ther.*
3. Never sing an *r* before a consonant. The *r* should be silent (*e.g., fortitude*).
4. Never sing an *r* before a pause in words (i.e., any place the singer stops the sound for a breath to clarify text, a rest, or special emphasis for interpretation) or a silent letter, unless the silent letter is followed by a vowel sound.

Begin to immediately apply the basic rules and suggestions above to English texts performed in your choral ensemble or in solo auditions. Greater clarity, tone quality, and intelligibility will be the unmistakable result of your dedicated work.

LATIN DICTION (ROMAN PRONUNCIATION)

A vast majority of the choral repertoire include texts in Latin, especially the sacred choral texts of the Mass as well as numerous settings of other sacred texts.

The beauty of this lyric language lies in pure, rich vowel sounds coupled with the appropriate syllable stress within each word by the singer. The combination of syllable stress and purity of the vowel connects the listener emotionally to the sound while also conveying the character and meaning of the word.

How to Use the Language Charts

Each of the four foreign languages (Latin, Italian, German, and French) included in *The Choral Singer's Survival Guide* organizes the vowels and consonants separately to provide the singer with absolute clarity of sound through example and detailed description. Rules regarding diphthongs and glides cite specific examples and practices in each language. As English consonants are our point of reference for consonant sounds, exceptions to pronunciation are noted after each consonant listed. For example, a *t* [t] in Latin is pronounced with a softer sound than in English. This information, in addition to a description of correct pronunciation, appears after the listed consonant.

To figure out the correct pronunciation of a word in any language, simply combine the correct vowel sound or combination with the consonant sounds, following the rules for each consonant sound and you'll have it.

For instance, take the word *scuto*, in Latin. If we break it apart, we know from our consonant chart that *sc* before *a, o, u,* or *h* is pronounced *sk* [sk] as in <u>sc</u>hool, the *u* is always pronounced [u] *oo*, the *t* [t] is pronounced as it is in English but softened slightly, and the *o* is always pronounced [ɔ] *aw*. Put those sounds together and you have skOO-taw [skutɔ]. You will be a pro in no time with some practice!

Latin Vowels

Latin vowels are warm, open sounds, and the singer should produce a pure, resonant, unchanging vowel sound combined with appropriate syllable stress for forward motion of the phrase. Stressed syllables are capitalized in the nonphonetic transcription and underlined in all IPA examples.

Spelling	Pronunciation	Example
a	[a] *ah* (f<u>a</u>ther)	P<u>a</u>ter (pAH-tehr) [pat̪ɛɾ]
e, ae, oe	[ɛ] *eh* (s<u>e</u>t)	R<u>e</u>x (rEH-ks) [rɛks]
i	[i] *ee* (s<u>ee</u>)	<u>i</u>n (een) [<u>i</u>n]
o	[ɔ] *aw* (f<u>ou</u>ght)	D<u>o</u>mine (dAW mee-neh) [d<u>ɔ</u>minɛ]
u	[u] *oo* (m<u>oo</u>n)	l<u>u</u>x (lOOks) [l<u>u</u>ks]
y	[i] *ee* (s<u>ee</u>) mostly in Greek words	K<u>y</u>rie (kEE-ree-eh) [k<u>i</u>ɾiɛ]

When consecutive vowels appear within a word, each vowel retains its own distinct sound and is treated as a separate syllable: *Filii* (fEE-lee-ee) [f<u>i</u>lii].

Syllable Stress in Latin

All two-syllable words in Latin have the stress on the first syllable. In multisyllable words, the stressed vowel is underlined as a guide to the reader. As you perform more and more texts in Latin, you will begin to easily identify the stress and release of syllables within the language.

Diphthongs in Latin

Diphthongs in Latin are sounded <u>only</u> when they are spelled out within a word. Otherwise, they are forbidden. For instance, *Dei* is pronounced dEH-ee [dɛi], and *te* [tɛ] is never pronounced "tay." To avoid the diphthong in single vowel sounds like *te*, maintain an open space throughout the duration of the vowel. The exception to the rule above occurs when the digraphs æ and œ are present in a word. In this case, the two vowels sound together as one sound, [ɛ] *eh*.

The most common diphthongs in Latin are *ai, au, ay, ei, eu, ou, ui, ue, ua,* and *uo: mei* (mEH-ee) [mɛi]; *tua* (tOO-ah) [tua].

Whereas the first six diphthongs give the first vowel the most emphasis in the word, when the *u* is preceded by *q* or *ng* and followed by another vowel, the stress is placed on the second vowel, creating a glide: *qui* (kwEE) [kwi].

Latin Consonants

Consonants should be pronounced with a quick, sharp articulation. However, the consonants *d, t,* and *k* should be softened slightly. Double consonants should be prolonged (as in Italian) and exaggerated slightly.

Spelling	Pronunciation	Example
b	pronounced as in English	bonae (bAW-neh) [bɔnɛ]
c (before *a, o, u,* or *h*)	*k* [k]	Christe (krEE-steh) [kristɛ]
c (before *e, i, y, ae,* or *oe*)	*ch* [tʃ] as in church	coeli (chEH-lee) [tʃɛli]
c (at the end of a word)	generally pronounced *k* [k]	haec (EHk) [ɛk]
cc (before *e, i, y, ae,* or *oe*)	pronounced *tch* [tʃ] as in hatch	ecce (EH-tcheh) [ɛtʃɛ]
d	pronounced as in English, yet the sound should be softened by a downward stroke of the tongue from behind the upper teeth to articulate this consonant	Dei (dEH-ee) [dɛi]
f	pronounced as in English	filium (fEE-lee-oom) [filium]

Spelling	Pronunciation	Example
g (before *e, i, y, ae*, or *oe*)	[dʒ] as in genius	Regina (reh-jEE-nah)[rɛdʒina]
g (except after *n*)	*g* [g] as in go	Gloria (glAW-ree-ah) [glɔria]
gn	pronounced like the *ny* [ɲ] sound in onion	magnum (mAH-nyoom) [maɲum]
h	silent with the exception of two words—*mihi* and *nihil*—where the *h* is pronounced like a *k* [k]	mihi (mEE-kɛɛ) [miki]
j	often written as an *i*, is pronounced [i] *ee*. This consonant "glides" into vowels following it. Move through the [i] *ee* sound very quickly into the vowel that follows.	ejus (EH-yoos) [ɛjus]
k	pronounced as in English, but softened slightly	kalendae (kah-lEHn-deh) [kalɛndɛ]
l	articulated with the tip of the tongue, not the back of the tongue	lauda (lAH-oo-dah) [lauda]
m	pronounced as in English	mater (mAH-tehr) [matɛr]

(Continued)

Spelling	Pronunciation	Example
n	pronounced as in English. However, as with the consonants *d* and *t*, *n* should be articulated with a sharp downward stroke of the tongue from behind the upper teeth.	nobis (nAW-bees) [nɔbis]
p	pronounced as in English	pax (pAHks) [paks]
ph	*f* [f]	phonascus (faw-nAH-skoos) [fɔnaskus]
q	pronounced like *k* [k]. However, since this consonant is usually followed by a *u*, which acts as a glide to the next vowel (see diphthongs above), the *k* sound must be crisp, moving quickly to the primary vowel sound.	qui (kwEE) [kwi]
r	rolled at the beginning of a word and flipped slightly in the middle or end of a word. However, maintain the integrity of the vowel and do not roll or flip the *r* too early.	Rex (rEH-ks) [rɛks]
s	pronounced as in English, except when it appears between two vowels. In that case, the *s* is softened slightly.	sicut (sEE-koot) [sikut]

Spelling	Pronunciation	Example
sc (before e, i, y, ae, oe, or eu)	pronounced sh [ʃ] as in <u>sh</u>ine	sceptrum (shEH-ptroom) [ʃɛptɾum]
sc (before a, o, u, or h)	pronounced sk [sk] as in <u>sch</u>ool	paschali (pah-skAH-lee) [pask<u>a</u>li]
t (at the beginning of a word)	pronounced as in English. However, as with the consonant d, the sound is executed with a sharp stroke of the tongue, making it less percussive than an English t.	tibi (tEE-bee) [t<u>i</u>bi]
th	pronounced t [t]	catholicam (kah-tAW-lee-kahm) [kat<u>ɔ</u>likam]
ti (before a vowel and following any letter except for s, t, or x)	pronounced tsee [tsi]	deprecationem (deh-prɛh-kah-tsee-AW-nehm) [dɛprɛkatsi<u>ɔ</u>nɛm]
ti (following s, t, or x)	pronounced tee [ti]	modestia (maw-dEH-stee-ah) [mɔdɛstia]
v	pronounced as in English	victimae (vEE-ktee-meh) [v<u>i</u>ktimɛ]
x	pronounced ks [ks] as in mar<u>ks</u>	Rex (rEHks) [ɾ<u>ɛ</u>ks]

(Continued)

Spelling	Pronunciation	Example
x (between two vowels or at the beginning of a word when the *x* is preceded by an *e* or followed by an *s* or *h*)	pronounced *gz* [gz]	exaudi (eh-gzAHoo-di) [ɛgzaudi]
xc (before *e, i, y, ae,* or *oe*)	pronounced *ksh* [kʃ]	Excelsis (eh-kshEHl-sees) [ɛkʃɛlsis]
xc (before *a, o,* or *u*)	*ksk* [ksk]	excanto (ehks-kAHn-taw) [ɛkskantɔ]
z	pronounced like *dz* [dz] as in bi<u>ds</u>	Lazaro (lAH-dzah-raw) [ladzarɔ]

ITALIAN DICTION

From the Italian madrigal of the Renaissance to the great choral operas such as Verdi's *Nabucco*, the Italian language has played a pivotal role in the development of singers for many years and continues to do so today. The famous *bel canto* (beautiful singing) technique that emerged in the 16th century is still taught in some form in vocal studios around the world. Bel canto technique offers the singer a consistent tone from the very lowest note in the range to the highest without "breaks" in the voice. This fluidity of line in bel canto singing is directly linked to the purity of the five vowels and seven vowel sounds of the Italian language.

Italian Vowels

Spelling	Pronunciation	Example
a	[a] *ah* (f<u>a</u>ther)	amore (ah-MOH-reh) [am<u>o</u>rɛ]
e	[e] similar to m<u>ay</u>, but without a diphthong	questo (qwAY-staw) [kw<u>e</u>stɔ]
e, è	[ɛ] *eh* (s<u>e</u>t)	deh (dEH) [dɛ]
i	[i] *ee* (s<u>ee</u>)	vidi (vEE-dee) [v<u>i</u>di]
o	[o] *oh* (b<u>oa</u>t)	voce [v<u>o</u>tʃɛ] (vOH-cheh) [v<u>o</u>tʃɛ]
o, ò	[ɔ] *aw* (<u>a</u>we)	ristoro (ree-stAW-raw) [rist<u>ɔ</u>rɔ]
u	[u] *oo* (m<u>oo</u>n)	luna (lOO-nah) [l<u>u</u>na]

Italian spelling in the musical score does not indicate open (short) or closed (long) pronunciation for *e* and *o*; they are the only two vowels in Italian that have both an open (short) and closed (long) pronunciation. However, there are a few simple rules to help the singer determine when to open or close a vowel in Italian.

1. Final *e* and *o* are open (short): *caro* (kAH-raw) [k<u>a</u>rɔ].
2. Unstressed *e* and *o* are open (short) in words with more than one syllable: *fortuna* (fawr-tOO-nah) [fɔrt<u>u</u>na].
3. A grave accent (*è* or *ò*) opens the vowel sound: *è* [ɛ] *eh*.
4. In other circumstances, *e* or *o* may be either open (short) or closed (long). The singer should consult an Italian dictionary to verify the correct sound.

Elision in Italian

An apostrophe is used to indicate elision in Italian. An unstressed final vowel is dropped and the consonant is elided to the vowel of the following word. The apostrophe unites the words rather than separating them. Simply pronounce every letter as if the apostrophe is not there: *una aura* becomes *un'aura* [unauɾa].

Syllable Stress in Italian

As a general rule, syllable stress within a word falls on the penultimate (next to last) syllable. In a two-syllable word, the stress would then fall on the first syllable.

An easy indicator of word stress is the grave accent. As noted above, a grave accent over an *e* or *o* (*è* or *ò*) opens the vowel sound. However, the grave accent over a final *a*, *i*, or *u* (*à*, *ì*, or *ù*) does not open the vowel, for these open vowel sounds do not exist in Italian. The accent in all cases indicates that the stress of the word falls on the final vowel sound.

è [ɛ] *eh; può* (pwAW) [pwɔ]　　　The grave accent opens the vowel and, in the
　　　　　　　　　　　　　　　　　second example, opens the vowel and indicates
　　　　　　　　　　　　　　　　　stress on the final syllable.

servitù (sehr-vee-tOO) [sɛɾvitu]　　The grave accent indicates word stress on the final
　　　　　　　　　　　　　　　　　vowel, but does not open the vowel sound.

Glides in Italian

Whenever an *i* or *u* shares one musical note with a vowel that follows, they become a glide to the next vowel sound.

quasi (kwAH-zee) [kwazi]　　　　*Guido* (gwEE-daw) [gwido]

Diphthongs and Triphthongs

As in Latin, diphthongs are spelled out in Italian. However, in the Italian language, triphthongs (three vowel sounds in succession) are more common. Again, the syllable stress for most words will fall on the penultimate syllable and in the case of a triphthong will usually fall on the next to last vowel.

Diphthong	*lui* (lOO-ee) [l<u>ui</u>]	
Triphthong	*tuoi* (twAW-ee) [tw<u>ɔi</u>]	

Italian Consonants

Double consonants in the Italian language receive double time and should be pronounced with intensity. One can innocently change the meaning of the text through overlooking the double consonants in Italian words. *Anno*, or year, has a very different meaning from *ano*, for example. Intensify double consonants always wherever they appear in a word. If a pair of double consonants is used in a word, make sure to exaggerate both pairs. A colon is used below in the nonphonetic and phonetic examples to remind the singer to intensify double consonants.

Tip: Lengthen the vowel sound to avoid pronouncing a single consonant as a double consonant.

Spelling	Pronunciation	Example
b	pronounced as in English	bella (bEHI:lah) [bɛl:la]
c (before *e* or *i*)	*ch* [tʃ] as in <u>ch</u>urch	ci (chEE) [tʃi]
c (before *a, o, u, h,* or any consonant)	*k* [k], not aspirated	che (kEH) [kɛ]
d	pronounced as in English, yet the sound should be softened by stroking the tip of the tongue against the upper gum ridge to articulate this consonant	dolce (dOHI-cheh) [d<u>o</u>ltʃɛ]
f	pronounced as in English	flutti (flOOt:ti) [fl<u>u</u>t:ti]
g (before *e* or *i*)	pronounced [dʒ] as in judge	gentile (jehn-tEE-leh) [dʒɛnti̲lɛ]

(Continued)

Spelling	Pronunciation	Example
g (before *a*, *o*, *u*, *h*, or any consonant)	*g* [g] as in go	gamba (gAHm-bah) [gamba]
gli	can be compared to the sound "lyee." The sound is made with a <u>single</u> movement of the front of the tongue against the front of the hard palate. This sound should not be confused with the [lj] glide in the English word mil<u>li</u>on, which requires two different movements of the tongue.	figlio (fEE-yaw) [fiʎɔ]
gn	pronounced like the *ny* [ɲ] sound in o<u>ni</u>on. The sound is made with the middle of the tongue.	signore (see-NYOH-reh) [siɲɔrɛ]
h	always silent	hanno (AHn:naw) [an:nɔ]
l	articulated with the tip of the tongue, not the back of the tongue	lunga (lOOng-gah) [luŋga]
m	pronounced as in English	mio (mEE-aw) [miɔ]
n	pronounced as in English. However, as with the consonants *d* and *t*, *n* should be articulated with a sharp downward stroke of the tongue from behind the upper teeth.	non (nOHn) [non]
n (before *g*, *c*, or *qu*)	*ng* [ŋ] as in ri<u>ng</u>	languir (lahng-gWEEr) [laŋgwir]

Spelling	Pronunciation	Example
p	pronounced as in English, but not as explosive as an English *p*	petto (pEHt:taw) [pɛt:tɔ]
qu	pronounced like *kw* [kw]. As in Latin, the *u* acts as a glide to the next vowel. The *k* sound must be crisp, moving quickly through the *u* to the primary vowel sound.	questo (qwAY-staw) [kwestɔ]
r	rolled at the beginning of a word or preceding a consonant and flipped between two vowels. However, maintain the integrity of the vowel and do not roll or flip the *r* too early.	caro (kAH-raw) [karɔ]
s	pronounced as in English	stella (stEHl:lah) [stɛl:la]
s (between two vowels)	*z* [z]	viso (VEE-zaw) [vizɔ]
sc (before *e* or *i*)	*sh* [ʃ] as in s<u>h</u>ine	scena (shEH-nah) [ʃɛna]
sc (before *a, o, u, h,* or any consonant)	*sk* [sk] as in <u>sc</u>hool	scala (skAH-lah) [skala]
t (at the beginning of a word)	pronounced as in English. However, the sound is executed with a sharp stroke of the tongue, making is less percussive than an English *t*. A final *t* does not occur in Italian.	tutto (tOOt:taw) [tut:tɔ]

(Continued)

Spelling	Pronunciation	Example
v	pronounced as in English	vino (vEE-naw) [vino]
z	may be pronounced as *ts* [ts] as in hi<u>ts</u> (unvoiced) or as *dz* [dz] in bi<u>ds</u> (voiced). There is no rule to determine when *z* is voiced or unvoiced. The singer will need to consult an Italian dictionary.	danza (dAHn-tsah) [dantsa] zero (dzEH-raw) [dzεro]

GERMAN DICTION

From Johann Sebastian Bach, possibly the greatest composer of all time, to Schubert, Schütz, Mendelssohn, and Distler, to the pinnacle of romantic choral music, *Ein Deutsches Requiem* by Johannes Brahms, German choral music continues to thrill audiences the world over.

German, which is often thought by some to be too "guttural" for singing, is actually a rich, warm language containing vowel sounds that will add resonance to the singer's voice when studied.

German Vowels

Spelling	Pronunciation	Example
a, aa, ah	[a] *ah* (f<u>a</u>ther)	tragen [tragən]
a	[ɒ] *ah* (h<u>o</u>t)	daß [dɒs]
ä, äh	[e] similar to m<u>ay</u>, but without a diphthong	säen [zeən]
ä, äeh	[ɛ] *eh* (s<u>e</u>t)	Bächlein [bɛçlaɪn]

Spelling	Pronunciation	Example
e	[e] similar to m<u>ay</u>, but without a diphthong	selig [ze<u>l</u>ɪç]
e	[ɛ] *eh* (s<u>e</u>t)	Herz [h<u>ɛ</u>rts]
e	[ə] (see "The Schwa in German" below)	Himmel [hɪ<u>m</u>:məl]
i, ie, ieh, ih	[i] *ee* (s<u>ee</u>)	ihnen [<u>i</u>nən]
i	[ɪ] *ih* (s<u>i</u>t)	sind [zɪnt]
o	[o] *oh* (b<u>oa</u>t)	Rote [r<u>o</u>tə]
o	[ɔ] *aw* (f<u>ou</u>ght)	sollen [z<u>ɔ</u>l:lən]
ö, öeh, öh	[ø] closed e [e] on the inside through a closed o [o] lip position	trösten [tr<u>ø</u>stən]
ö, oe	[œ] open e [ɛ] on the inside through an open o [ɔ] lip position	plötzlich [pl<u>œ</u>tslɪç]
u, uh	[u] *oo* (m<u>oo</u>n)	Blume [bl<u>u</u>mə]
u	[ʊ] (f<u>oo</u>t)	und [<u>ʊ</u>nt]
ü, üeh, üh	[y] closed i [i] on the inside through a closed u [u] lip position	Brüder [br<u>y</u>dər]
ü, ue	[ʏ] open i [ɪ] on the inside through an open u [ʊ] lip position	würdig [v<u>ʏ</u>rdɪç]

The Schwa in German

The vowel *e* becomes a schwa [ə] in the following situations:

1. The vowel is final or paired with a consonant or consonant pair: *tragen* [tɾagən]; *Freude* [fɾɔødə].
2. *E* is in the prefixes *ge-* and *be-*: *getröstet* [gətɾœstət]; *bebaut* [bəbaʊt].
3. The word combination contains the unstressed *e* sound: *Morgenregen* [mɔrgənregən].

Long or Short Vowels Sounds

A vowel sound is long in German when it is doubled, followed by an *h*, or follows a single consonant or single consonant followed by another vowel: *gehen* [geən].

A vowel sound is short in German when it follows two or more consonants. In addition, one-syllable words such as *an*, *das*, *es*, *in*, *mit*, and *von* are pronounced with a short vowel sound.

There are, of course, exceptions to the rules stated above. The singer should consult a German dictionary to determine the correct pronunciation. Langenscheidt's *Pocket German Dictionary*, which uses the IPA, is one such resource.

Syllable Stress in German

In general, the first syllable of words in German receives the most stress with the following exceptions:

1. The stress will fall on the second syllable in words beginning with *be-*, *ge-*, *end-*, *er-*, *ver-*, and *zer-*: *erfreuen* [ɛrfɾɔøən].
2. The stress will fall on the second syllable when the compound adverbs, *da*, *her*, *hin*, or *wo*, appear as the first syllable: *wohin* [vohɪn].

Diphthongs in German

There are three diphthong sounds in German.

1. *ei*, *ai*, *ay*, and *ey* resemble the final *ie* [aɪ] in the word p**ie**: *sein* [zaɪn].
2. *au* resembles the *ow* [aʊ] sound in the word c**ow**: *Posaune* [pozaʊnə].
3. *eu* and *äu* resemble the final *oy* [ɔø] in the word b**oy**: *Freuden* [fɾɔødən].

German Consonants

Consonants in German are quick and crisp and must be pronounced with absolute clarity. Double consonants should be suspended slightly, but not to the same degree as in Italian. A colon separates double consonants in the examples below.

Do not elide final consonants at the end of a word to a vowel beginning of a new word: Aber / ich not aberich.

Spelling	Pronunciation	Example
b	pronounced as in English	bist [bɪsl]
b (at the end of a word or syllable)	*p* [p]	habt [hɒpt]
c (at the beginning of a word)	*k* [k]	Chor [koɾ]
ch, ig (after *e, i*, consonants or mixed vowels)	[ç] spoken in the front of the mouth. The singer should feel air glide over the middle of the tongue. With the tip of the tongue behind the lower teeth, say the word "human" with intensity. *Ch* is never pronounced *ish* or *ik*.	mich [mɪç]
ch (at the end of the word or following *a, o, u*, or *au*)	[x] spoken in the back of the mouth, but should not sound like throat clearing. The back of the tongue lifts toward the soft palate, creating a sound of "friction" as the air passes between the tongue and soft palate.	ach [ɒx]
ck	*k* [k]	sticken [ʃtɪkən]

(Continued)

Spelling	Pronunciation	Example
d	pronounced as in English	der [de̲r]
d (at the end of a word or syllable)	*t* [t]	Tod [to̲t]
ds	*ts* [ts] as in bi<u>ts</u>	abends [a̲bənts]
f	pronounced as in English	Feierlich [fa̲ɪərlɪç]
g	pronounced as in English	gehen [ge̲ən]
g (at the end of a word or syllable, except after an *i* or *n*.	*k* [k]	Tag [to̲k]
g (following an *i*)	[ç] see *ch, ig* above	Geduldig [gədu̲ldɪç]
h	pronounced as in English	Himmel [hɪm:məl]
j	like *y* [j] in English	Jauchzen [ja̲ʊxtsən]
k	pronounced as in English	klein [kla̲ɪn]
l	produced with the <u>tip</u> of the tongue, not the back	willen [vɪ̲l:ən]
m, mm	pronounced as in English	Ruhm [ru̲m]
n, nn	pronounced as in English	neue [nɔ̲øə]
ng (within the same syllable)	pronounced as in English	singet [zɪŋət]

Spelling	Pronunciation	Example
ng (if the *n* and *g* belong to separate syllables or appear at the end of the first part of a compound word)	pronounced separately as *n* [n] and *g* [g]	Schwanengesang [ʃvanəngəzɒŋ]
p	pronounced as in English	Posaune [pozaʊnə]
ph	*f* [f]	Phantasie [fʊntɒzi]
qu	*kv* [kv]	Qualen [kvalən]
r	flipped or rolled for dramatic emphasis	Ruh [ru]
s (followed by a vowel)	*z* [z]	sind [zɪnt]
s (followed by a consonant)	*sh* [ʃ]	Schmerz [ʃmɛrts]
s (at the end of a word or syllable)	*s* [s]	wildes [vɪldəs]
ss or **ß** (*das Eszett* or *scharfes S* – sharp *s*)	represents a double *ss* and may be written either as an *ss* or ß, indicating that the preceding vowel is long. *Das Eszett* is used at the end of a word, whether the preceding vowel is long or short.	daß [dɒs]
sch	pronounced *sh* [ʃ]	Schatten [ʃɒt:tən]
st (at the beginning of a word of syllable)	pronounced *sht* [ʃt]	Stachel [ʃtɒxəl]

(Continued)

Spelling	Pronunciation	Example
th	*t* [t]	Thron [tr<u>o</u>n]
ts	*ts* [ts]	nichts [n<u>ɪ</u>çts]
tz	*ts* [ts]	besitzen [bəz<u>ɪ</u>tsən]
v	*f* [f]	vogellieder [f<u>o</u>gəlːlidər]
w	*v* [v]	wieder [v<u>i</u>dər]
z, zz	*ts* [ts] as in ge<u>ts</u>	Herz [h<u>ɛ</u>rts]

FRENCH DICTION

L'Académie Française (the French Academy), founded in 1635 by the Cardinal de Richelieu, oversees the correct usage and pronunciation of the French language. The French Academy is composed of 40 members—including poets, doctors, scientists, philosophers, clergy, and artists—called *Les immortels* (the immortals). Members of the French Academy are elected by their peers for life and may not resign unless asked to do so by their fellow academy members. Election to *L'Académie Française* is considered a very high honor.

For most singers, French is the most difficult language to grasp in a choral rehearsal or a college diction class. Part of the challenge, as is the case with many English words, is learning what <u>not</u> to pronounce. The other challenge lies in learning the correct pronunciation of the nasal vowels and the difference between a pure [u] and [y].

You will notice immediately that the French diction section is almost twice as long as those of other languages. The goal is to provide you with the most complete information possible in a nonintimidating format, to diminish the fear of learning to sing in French.

The vowels are separated below into nonnasal and nasal categories. In addition, you will find other spellings located under each nonnasal vowel sound. These sounds will be pronounced exactly as the vowel sound indicates in the chart when they appear within a word.

With a bit of focused practice and patience, you will be able to grasp the French language for singing. This command of the language will be employed fully in master choral works such as *Cantique de Jean Racine* by Gabriel Fauré, *Trois Chansons de Charles d'Orléans* by Claude Debussy, and Arthur Honegger's *Le Roi David*.

Syllable Stress in French

In French, there are no stress marks in words, and all syllables are pronounced with the same intensity. The exception is the last syllable of a long word or a group of words, which is not stressed but simply has a longer duration. French rhythm patterns (*groupes rythmiques*) produce a flowing musical line that will help you create forward motion in phrasing when fully applied.

French Vowels

French Nonnasal Vowels

Spelling	Pronunciation	Example
a also *a* before *s* or *z* and *a* before final silent *s*	[a] *ah* (f<u>a</u>ther)	âme [am]
a, à, oi	[ɒ] *ah* (h<u>o</u>t)	Madame [mɒdam]
e, ed, eil, er, et, ez also final *ai, e* before a final silent consonant (except *s* and *t*), *es* (in monosyllables)	[e] similar to m<u>ay</u>, but without a diphthong	été [ete]

(Continued)

Spelling	Pronunciation	Example
e, ê, es, est also *e* before a pronounced final consonant, *e* before two or more consonants, *ai, aî, aie, aient, ei, ey, e* before a silent *t*	[ɛ] *eh* (s<u>e</u>t)	père [pɛr]
eu, eû, eux also *eu* as a final sound, *eu* before *z*	[ø] closed *e* [e] on the inside through a closed *o* [o] lip position	deux [dø]
eu	[œ] open *e* [ɛ] on the inside through an open *o* [ɔ] lip position	fleur [flœr]
i, î, ï, y	[i] *ee* (s<u>ee</u>)	ici [isi]
o, ô also *au, aux, eau,* and *eaux*; *o* as the final sound in a word; *o* before a *z* sound (typically an *s* between two vowels)	[o] *oh* (b<u>o</u>at)	nos [no]
o also *au* before *r*	[ɔ] *aw* (f<u>ou</u>ght)	porte [pɔrt]

Spelling	Pronunciation	Example
ou, oux also *oû, où, oue* at the end of a word or syllable	[u] *oo* (m<u>oo</u>n)	jour [ʒuɾ]
u also *û* and *ue* at the end of a word or syllable	[y] closed *i* [i] on inside through a closed *u* [u] lip position	du [dy]

The Schwa (e muet)

Although the schwa (*e muet*) is usually not pronounced at the end of words in spoken French, it is very often pronounced as a final syllable in sung French. If the syllable contains a final *e* or ends in a third-person-plural verb ending (e.g., *parlent* [paɾlə]). The schwa symbol [ə] is not included in the examples below unless it is necessary for spoken pronunciation. However, you must remember to include the sound when the text calls for it.

The schwa, sounded as the *e* in th<u>e</u>, with very round lips, is always written <u>without an accent mark</u> and may appear:

1. As a final *e*, except when followed by a word beginning with a vowel or a mute *h*: *que* [kə]
2. At the end of a word after a double consonant or cluster of consonants: *prendre* [pɾɑ̃dɾə]
3. In the middle of a word to separate two consonants, generally before a single consonant followed by a vowel: *petit* [pət<u>i</u>]
4. In third-person-plural verb endings before *nt*: *parlent* [paɾlə]

In the nine single-syllable words (*ce, de, je, le, me, ne, que, se, te*), the final *e* is dropped, or elided, when it precedes a vowel or a mute *h*: *le* + *ami* = *l'ami* [lami]; *je* + *habite* = *j'habite* [ʒabit].

French Nasal Vowels

A vowel becomes nasal in French whenever an *m* or an *n* is final or precedes another consonant (e.g., *garçon* [gaʁsõ]; *prendre* [pʁãdʁə]). However, when singing nasal vowels it is important to use full resonance, allowing some air to pass through the mouth. If air passes through the nose only, the resulting sound will be unpleasant and inappropriate for singing.

To produce a beautiful nasal vowel, say the word *pond*. Now try to say the word without pronouncing the *nd*. In other words, do not move the tongue to articulate the *n*. A nasal vowel will result. The *n* space is where the nasality will occur in all vowel sounds. To pronounce the nasal vowel correctly, open for the appropriate vowel sound in the chart without moving the tongue and without pronouncing the *n*. The consonant that follows a nasal vowel should never be pronounced. Remember, the air should pass through both the mouth and the nose for a beautiful sound. A double *mm* or *nn* cancels nasality.

The French language has four nasal vowel sounds. Following the directions in the paragraph above, practice speaking each of the nasal vowels, using the keyword indicated for each. Once you have established the correct sound, take out the consonant sound that precedes the nasal vowel and practice speaking the nasal vowel only.

Spelling	Pronunciation	Example
am, an **em, en**	[ã] *ah(n)* (p<u>o</u>nd)	dans [dã]
aim, ain **eim, ein,** **im, in**	[ɛ̃] *eh(n)* (b<u>e</u>nt)	cinq [sɛ̃k]
om, on	[õ] *aw(n)* (h<u>au</u>nt)	garçon [gaʁsõ]
um, un	[œ̃] *uh(n)* (h<u>u</u>nt)	un [œ̃]

Diphthongs

Nonnasal Glides

Whenever *i, u,* or *ou* appears before another vowel, the first vowel sound moves quickly to the second vowel sound, creating a glide: *suis* [swi̯].

Exceptions:

1. When *e* is final: *vie* [vi]
2. When *e* precedes a final *s*: *moues* [muə]
3. In third-person-plural verb forms where *e* precedes the final *nt*: *parlent* [paʀlə]
4. Before a consonant and vowel combination: *reniement* [ʀɔnimã]

One of the most difficult glides (also a diphthong) in the French language is the *mouillé*, which may be written as *il* or *ill*. The sound is very similar in pronunciation to the *y* [j] in the English word *yet*. This sound occurs when:

1. A vowel precedes final *il*: *sommeil* [sɔmɛj]. However, if *il* appears before a vowel elsewhere, the *l* sound is pronounced as an *l*: *voile* [vwɒlɛ].
2. *Ill* appears after a consonant and in front of a vowel: *fille* [fij]. However, there are exceptions; please consult a dictionary.
3. *Ill* appears between two vowels: *cailloux* [kaju].

Tip: *Oi, oix,* and *oy* (in some cases) are pronounced *wah* [wa]: *soir* [swɒʀ].

Nasal Glides

There are two nasal glides in French. The nasal glide *ie* appears in words like *bien* [bjɛ̃]. As with all glides, move quickly through the [j] sound into the nasal vowel. As a reminder, this nasal vowel is pronounced like *eh(n)* in the word *bent*.

The other nasal glide sound is *oin* and *oim*: *point* [pwɛ̃]. This glide is a combination of a quick *w* sound moving to the nasal *eh(n)* sound described above.

Triphthongs

Along with the two-vowel diphthongs in the nonnasal and nasal glides above, a three-vowel triphthong also appears quite often in French. *Euil*, *euille*, *ueil*, and *ueille* are pronounced [œj]: *accueil* [akœj].

Correct pronunciation of this sound is particularly challenging for English speakers.

French Consonants

Spelling	Pronunciation	Example
b, bb	pronounced as in English	bonne [bɔn]
c (before *e*, *i*, or *y*)	*s* [s]	cette [sɛt]
c, cc (before *a, o, u,* or a consonant)	*k* [k]	comme [kɔm]
ç	*s* [s] and only occurs before *a, o,* or *u*	garçon [garsõ]
ch	*sh* [ʃ] in s<u>h</u>ine	riche [riʃ]
d, dd	pronounced as in English	dans [dã]
f, ff	pronounced as in English	fille [fij]
g (before *e, i,* or *y*)	like the *s* [ʒ] in vi<u>s</u>ion	gens [ʒã]
g (before *a, o,* or *u*)	*g* [g]	garçon [garsõ]
gn	like the *ny* [ɲ] of ca<u>ny</u>on	ligne [liɲə]
h (*h muet*)	silent	homme [ɔm]
h (*h aspiré*)	silent	haut [o]

Spelling	Pronunciation	Example
j	like the *s* [ʒ] in vi<u>s</u>ion	jardin [ʒaʁdɛ̃]
k	pronounced as in English, but very uncommon in French	ski [ski]
l, ll	*l* [l] except when they follow an i (see *l mouillé*)	livre [livʁə]
m, mm	pronounced as in English	maison [mɛzõ]
n, nn	pronounced as in English	notre [nɔtʁə]
p, pp	pronounced as in English	petit [pəti]
q (final consonant)	*k* [k]	cinq [sɛ̃k]
qu	*k* [k]	quatre [katʁə]
r	slightly flipped, as in Italian	rue [ʁu]
s, ss	*s* [s]	laisser [lɛse]
s (between two vowels)	*z* [z]	bise [biz]
s (at the end of a word)	usually silent	très [tʁɛ]
t	pronounced as in English	tous [tu]
t (before an *i* followed by a vowel)	*s* [s]	nation [nasjõ]
tch	*ch* [tʃ] as in <u>ch</u>urch	Tchad [tʃad]
th	*t* [t]	thé [te]
v	pronounced as in English	vous [vu]

(Continued)

Spelling	Pronunciation	Example
w	usually pronounced *w* [w]. All words with a *w* are borrowed from other languages.	Watt [wat]
w	pronounced like a *v* [v] in foreign words	wagon [vagõ]
x (before most consonants)	*ks* [ks] in boo<u>ks</u>	exciter [ɛksite]
x (before most vowels)	*gz* [gz] in le<u>gs</u>	exile [ɛgzil]
x (at the end of a word)	silent, except for the words *six* and *dix*, where the *x* is pronounced s̩ [s]	dix [dis]
y (after a consonant)	*ee* [i] in s<u>ee</u>	mythe [mit]
y (when followed by a vowel at the beginning of a word)	*y* [j] in y̱es	yeux [jø]
y (between two vowels)	*y* [j] in yes	royal [ɾwajal]
z	pronounced as in English	zèle [zɛl]

Tip: There are two kinds of *h's* (both are still silent)—the mute *h* (*h muet*) and the aspirate *h* (*h aspiré*). The majority of *h's* in French are mute. The word that follows a mute *h* acts as if it begins with a vowel sound, and liaison (see discussion of *liaison* following this list) and contractions are allowed. The aspirate *h* usually occurs in words borrowed from other languages. Liaison and contractions are not allowed before the aspirate *h*: *l'homme* [lɔm] (mute *h*); *très haut* [tɾɛ/o] (aspirate *h*).

> **Tip:** In conversational French, *r*'s are pronounced with a uvular trill (a trill produced by vibrations of the back of the tongue against or near the uvula). French singers and actors use the flipped *r* [ɾ] for sung French and formal stage performances.

Liaison

Liaison occurs in French when a consonant that would normally be silent is pronounced before a word beginning with a vowel or a mute *h*. There are three types of liaison: *required liaison*, *optional liaison*, and *forbidden liaison*. Because liaison can be very confusing, this topic concentrates only on forbidden liaison. Decisions regarding required and optional liaisons will be made by your conductor, who may consult with a language expert. In the majority of circumstances, it will be "safe" to use liaison except as indicated below.

Forbidden liaison occurs to avoid confusion with words or expressions that are similar in nature. Liaison should not be used in any of the following circumstances:

1. Before a word beginning with an aspirate *h*: *très haut* [tɾɛ / o]
2. After et: *et / ils chantent* [ɛ / il ʃãtə]
3. After a singular noun: *un garçon / est* [œ̃ gaɾsõ / ɛ]
4. Preceding *onze* and *oui*: *un / oui* [œ̃ / wi]
5. After a final *rd*, *rs*, and *rt*, except when a final *rs* indicates pluralization: *dort / un* [dɔɾ / œ̃]. The singer should link the *r* to the oncoming vowel rather than the *t*.
6. After interrogative expressions (questions) and a few adverbs: *Comment est-il?* [kõmõ / ɛ til]; *toujours ici* [tuʒuɾ / isi]
7. For syntactical separation, generally after punctuation in sung French, or when separation is needed to support the meaning of the text: *des amis, est mis* [de zami / ɛ mi]

The pronunciation of final *d*, *f*, *s*, and *x* are altered in liaison. *D* becomes a *t*, *f* becomes a *v*, and both *s* and *x* become *z*: *Quand est-ce que* [kã tɛ skœ]; *neuf heures* [nœ vœɾ]; *mes amis* [me zami].

Mute Final Consonants

Final *b* (preceded by *m*), *d*, *p* (before *t*), *ps*, *r* (following an *e*), *s*, *t*, *x*, and *z* are mute: *amis* [ami]; *yeux* [jø]; *petit* [pəti].

MUSICAL TERMS

Prior to the invention of the metronome about 1812, composers indicated tempo through the use of specific musical terms, first in Italian beginning around 1600, and then in German and French. Today, many musical expressions appear in English as well.

Tempo markings and metronome markings appear in the top left corner of the page at the beginning of the piece or at the beginning of each movement in a larger work.

GENERAL TEMPO TERMS FROM SLOWEST TO FASTEST

Italian	German	French	English
larghissimo	sehr langsam	très lent	as slow as possible
largo	breit	large	broadly, stately
larghetto	etwas langsam	un peu lent	faster than largo
grave	schwer	lourd	heavy, solemn
lento	langsam	lent	slow
adagio	getragen	lent	slow, but not as slow as largo, at ease
adagietto			not as slow as adagio
andante	gehend	allant	moderate walking speed
andantino			generally faster than andante
moderato	mässig	modéré	moderate
allegretto	etwas bewegt	un peu animé	not as fast as allegro
allegro	schnell	animé	fast, quick, rapid
vivace	lebhaft	vif	faster than allegro, lively
presto	eilig	rapide	very fast
prestissimo			as fast as possible

(Continued)

The suffix *–issimo* in Italian modifies the tempo mark in its own direction. The marking *larghissimo* means slowest, whereas *prestissimo* means fastest.

The suffixes *–ino* or *–etto* modify the tempo mark in the opposite of its direction. *Larghetto* means less slow or a bit faster than largo, and *allegretto* means less fast or slower than allegro.

TEMPO MODIFICATION TERMS

The following terms either modify the tempo at the beginning of the piece or movement or change the tempo within a section of the musical work.

Italian	German	French	English
a piacere			at the liberty of the performer
a tempo	erstes zeitmass	1er tempo	return to the original tempo
accelerando	schneller werden	accélerer	accelerate
allargando	verbreiten	enlargissant	broaden, slowing down
con	mit	avec	with
l'istesso tempo			same tempo, beat
lo stesso tempo			remains constant at a meter change
meno	weniger	moins	less
meno mosso	weniger bewegt	moins vite	less motion
molto	sehr	très	very
morendo	ersterben	en mourant	fading away in tempo and volume
non troppo	nicht zu	pas trop	not too much
più	the suffix -er	plus	more
più mosso	bewegter	plus animé	more motion
poco	ein wenig	un peu	little, somewhat
poco a poco	allmahlich	peu à peu	little by little
rallentando (rall.)	zurückhalten	ralentir	gradually slower
ritardando (rit.)			gradually slower
ritenuto	zurückgehalten	retenu	slow immediately

Italian	German	French	English
rubato			a relaxing or speeding up of the pulse
smorzando (smorz.)			sudden decrease in tempo and volume
stringendo	drängend	en pressant	pressing forward
subito	plötzlich	tout à coup	suddenly
tempo giusto			strict tempo
tempo primo	erstes zeitmass	premier tempo	return to the original tempo
tenuto			held, sustained
trattenuto (tratt.)		cédez	slight holding back of tempo, delayed

MUSICAL FORM TERMS

Term	Definition
al	to the, usually preceding *coda* or *fine*
attacca	go to the next section without a break
coda	the final section of the piece ⊕
da capo	from the beginning (D.C.)
dal segno	from the sign (D.S.) 𝄋
dal segno al coda	from the sign to the coda (D.S. al coda)
fermata	hold ⌢
fine	the end
1st or 2nd ending	repeat with different endings
repeat	repeat the section between the signs

GENERAL TERMS

Because the Italians were the first to use terms as a road map for musical expression and interpretation, the vast majority of musical terms appear in that language. German and Latin terms are identified as (Ger.) or (Lat.) below.

Term	Definition
a niente	to nothing
ad libitum (ad lib.) (Lat.)	at the liberty of the performer, or that the inclusion of a particular voice or instrument in the ensemble is optional
affettuoso	affectionately, with feeling
agitato	agitated, restless
alla breve	cut time; half note as unit
amoroso	lovingly, tenderly
animato	animated, lively
appassionato	with passion and emotion
assai	very, extremely
ben	well
cantabile	in a singing manner
come	like
con brio	with spirit
con calore	with warmth
con forza	with force
con fuoco	with fire, passion
con moto	with movement
cupo	dark
dolce	sweetly
dolcissimo	very sweetly
dolente	sadly
espressivo	with expression, feeling
giocoso	humorous, playful
grazioso	graceful
il	the
legato	smooth and connected
leggiero	light, graceful
ma	but
maestoso	majestic, dignified
marcato	marked or emphasized

Term	Definition
martellato	hammered
misterioso	mysterious
moderato	moderately
non	not
parlando	in a spoken manner
pesante	heavy
pochissimo	very little
quasi	almost, as if
ruhig (Ger.)	calm, peaceful
scherzando	playfully
secco	dry, detached
segue	go right on, continue in the same way
semplice	simply
sempre	always
senza	without
sforzando, sforzato (sfz., sf.)	a sudden, strong accent on a note or chord
simile	similarly, in like manner
sognando	dreamily
sostenuto	sustained
sotto voce	a subdued vocal sound
staccato	short and detached
subito	suddenly
tranquillo	tranquil, calm
tacet	do not sing
troppo	too much
tutti	all together, everyone
un	a, one, an
vivo	animated, quick
volti subito (v.s.)	turn the page immediately

KEY SIGNATURES

SHARPS

FLATS

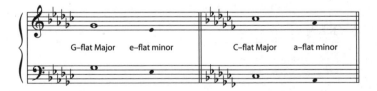

VOCAL RANGES AND CLASSIFICATIONS

VOICE CLASSIFICATIONS

Voices are classified based on four factors: range, quality, register changes ("lifts"), and tessitura.

Singers often believe that the highest or lowest note they can "reach" should determine their voice placement. *Range*, the gamut of pitches sung from lowest to highest, is an important factor. However, the conductor will listen for the most beautifully produced high and low notes when classifying a singer.

The *quality* of the voice—bright, dark, rich, lyric—is also a consideration when classifying voices. Vocal quality is heavily influenced by the singer's age and amount of vocal training.

The identification of *register changes* is helpful in classifying the voice, as there is an almost universal lift on F for high voices, E for medium voices, and D for lower voices (see figure 3.1 in Chapter 3). However, using this method to classify immature singers or those with little training is often unreliable without consideration of the other three factors.

The *tessitura* is the range of the voice containing the most beautiful, resonant, and easily produced tones; essentially, this refers to the singer's most comfortable range, and it is probably the single most important factor in voice classification.

Correct classification of singers' voices enhances the sound of the chorus and protects singers from potential vocal damage that can be caused by incorrect classification.

Vocal Ranges

The ranges below represent the average note-to-note ranges for soprano, alto, tenor, and bass voices. Individual singers may sing well above or below the pitches indicated.

R E S O U R C E

SIGHT-READING TIPS AND SUGGESTIONS

Singers often find sight-reading to be the most stressful part of their audition. Sight-reading ability becomes stronger with practice and repetition. To become a better sight-reader, you must simply practice reading music. Read your part of a hymn or Bach chorale. Also, see "Music Theory, Sight-Reading, and Music History" in Resource F: Online Choral Music Resources.

It is normal to make mistakes in the beginning; however, with focused practice you will find that you make fewer and fewer errors. As with vocal training, expect to "kiss a lot of frogs" before getting to the point where sight-reading becomes easy.

The following steps will help you improve your sight-reading ability in preparation for your audition:

1. Look at the key and meter of the piece. Glance at the first and last measure immediately to confirm the key. Is the piece in a major key or a minor key? Keep in mind that a piece may begin in major and move to minor, and vice versa. If you choose to read the piece using solfeggio, identify *do* or *la* to establish the tonality. See Resource C: Key Signatures.
2. Next, scan through the piece, paying special attention to challenging rhythms or intervals. Most errors occur because of incorrect rhythm. If time permits, isolate and practice the more challenging rhythms and intervals. You will have only a moment, so make the best use of your time.
3. Err on the slow side in choosing a tempo. Find sections with the fastest notes, and choose your tempo based on this information. It's easy to get off to a fast start in the excitement of the audition, but remember, the choice of tempo should be based on the quickest notes in the piece.
4. Note any accidentals, key changes, meter changes, or repeat signs occurring in the music. Also, be aware of interpretive markings in the music such as dynamics, crescendos, decrescendos, and musical terms.
5. Search for musical similarities. Are there patterns of notes that repeat in another section of the piece? Does an entire phrase or section repeat?

6. It is easy to miss repeated notes in music reading. Keep an eye out for them as you scan through the piece.
7. When you have finished your brief review of the music, take a slow, deep breath.
8. Sing the scale or tonic triad to establish the key in your ear.
9. Depending on the situation, you may be asked to sing with text or on a neutral vowel. If you are given the opportunity to choose the vowel, choose the one you are most comfortable singing.
10. As you sing, you may wish to tap lightly or conduct with your hand to maintain a steady pulse during the reading.
11. If you miss a note or rhythm, *keep going*. In your practice sessions, it's fine to stop and fix a note or rhythm to develop your skills. However, during an audition it's important to forge ahead and not let one missed note or rhythm throw you off for the entire piece.
12. Give yourself permission to make mistakes. It's really not the end of the world if you do. In fact, trying to be "perfect" may cause you to make more errors because of the added mental pressure.
13. Look ahead, focusing on complete ideas rather than one note at a time. Sing phrases.
14. In your reading, incorporate as much musicality as possible.

Sight-reading involves much more than just singing the correct notes. Read everything on the page, including dynamics, phrasing, articulation, and other expressive suggestions. If dynamics are not suggested, incorporate your own musical ideas into the piece. Make the piece your own. Take a deep breath, and go for it!

RESOURCE

ONLINE CHORAL MUSIC RESOURCES

INTERNATIONAL CHORAL NETWORKS

ChoralNet
www.choralnet.org

As an international and multilingual Internet resource for the choral profession, ChoralNet provides a central portal to online resources and communications for the global choral music community. ChoralNet is a project of three major choral organizations: the American Choral Directors Association (ACDA), the International Federation for Choral Music (IFCM), and Chorus America.

ChoralNet operates three primary mailing lists—Choralist, ChoralAcademe, and Choral-Talk—and a news group that lets choral musicians exchange ideas, make professional connections, and learn about choral music. ChoralNet has 14 forums (bulletin boards), some with e-mail options that provide a place to post job notices and auditions, as well as promote interaction among specialized choral communities such as students and those in Europe and Latin America. ChoralNet provides links to more than 4,000 chorus websites worldwide.

International Federation of Choral Music (IFCM)
www.ifcm.net

IFCM was founded in 1982 for the purpose of facilitating communication and exchange between choral musicians throughout the world. The organization is fulfilling its purpose through its world and regional symposia, conducting of master classes, World Youth Choir, Choral Music Database (Musica), ChoralNet website, World Choral Census, International Choral Bulletin, World Day of Choral Singing, and many other projects.

NATIONAL ORGANIZATIONS

American Choral Directors Association (ACDA)
www.acdaonline.com

Founded in 1959, ACDA is a not-for-profit music education organization whose central purpose is to promote excellence in choral music through performance, composition, publication, research, and teaching. In addition, ACDA strives through arts advocacy to elevate choral music's position in American society. ACDA membership consists of approximately 18,000 choral directors who represent more than one million singers across the United States.

Chorus America
www.chorusamerica.org

Founded in 1977, Chorus America serves the spectrum of professional, volunteer, children/youth, and symphony/opera choruses. To accomplish its mission, Chorus America provides information, publications, conferences, consulting, training programs, surveys, networking, and awards to support choruses in North America.

MENC: The National Association for Music Education
www.menc.org

The mission statement of MENC is to advance music education by encouraging the study and making of music by all. Founded in 1907 with 64 members, its membership has grown to more than 100,000, including active music teachers, university faculty and researchers, college students preparing to be teachers, high school honor society members, and MusicFriends, a membership program of MENC. Formerly the Music Educators National Conference, the association changed its name in 1998 to MENC: The National Association for Music Education to better reflect its mission.

PRIVATE VOICE STUDY

Classical Singer (CS)
www.classicalsinger.com

The premier magazine for classical singers, *Classical Singer* is the leader of the movement to expand the dramatic vocal talents for the enjoyment of people everywhere. The *CS* website is the online gathering spot for the classical singer community, carrying up-to-the-minute listings of auditions and competitions. More than 200 forums give singers a site where they can interact on a variety of subjects. *CS* also provides online directories of singers, performances, teachers, coaches, summer training programs, and much more.

National Association of Teachers of Singing, Inc. (NATS)
www.nats.org

NATS is the largest association of teachers of singing in the world. With more than 5,000 members, all of whom have pledged to uphold a professional Code of Ethics, NATS continues to encourage the highest standards of singing through excellence in teaching and the promotion of vocal education and research. To find a teacher in your area, go to "Find A Teacher" under FYI on the website

VoiceTeachers.com
www.voiceteachers.com

VoiceTeachers.com, a user-friendly Internet directory of teachers of singing, is designed to help singers find qualified voice teachers in their area.

MUSIC THEORY, SIGHT-READING, AND MUSIC HISTORY

DataDragon
www.datadragon.com/education/

DataDragon offers online tutorials and guides in music reading, music history, and musical genres. The site also contains a message board for asking musical questions, a guide to learning about musical instruments, and links to other music education sites.

eMusicTheory
www.emusictheory.com

eMusicTheory provides online tools for teachers and students of basic music theory. The student drills on the website may be practiced for free.

Ricci Adams's Musictheory.net
www.musictheory.net

This is a great site. You will learn scales, intervals, chords, key signatures, time signatures, note duration, and much more. For the more advanced student, a chord calculator is included as well as a matrix generator for those studying modern music. You can even print out your own customized staff paper.

teoría Music Theory web
www.teoria.com

Here you will find tutorials for learning about various aspects of music theory, exercises to practice and develop music theory and ear-training skills, and a reference section containing articles about music theory, music history, and analysis. The teoría site may be viewed in either English or Spanish.

SHEET MUSIC

J. W. Pepper
www.jwpepper.com

Founded in 1876, J. W. Pepper is now the world's largest sheet music retailer. Its catalog contains well over 400,000 titles for chorus, band, and orchestra, as well as materials for individual instruments.

Musical Resources of Toledo, Ltd.
www.musical-resources.com

Musical Resources has served the choral community since 1986, providing excellent service and high-quality resources for professional and amateur choral musicians.

SheetMusicPlus
www.sheetmusicplus.com

SheetMusicPlus contains almost 400,000 titles, including songbooks, scores, tabs, and instructional methods in a variety of genres that include choral, pop, classical, Broadway, and jazz.

MUSIC FOLDERS

The Black Folder
www.emersonenterprises.com for U.S. orders
www.musicfolder.com for international orders

This folder is "the world's best choral folder." Both standard and deluxe models are available and may be ordered directly from the website. A discount is offered for bulk orders. A removable ring adapter, double cords, and a transparent leaflet pocket may be added to the folder at an additional cost. You may also order the folder directly from Andrew Black, the creator of the folder, in Huntington Park, California, by calling (323) 588-9000.

UNION CONTACTS

American Federation of Television and Recording Artists (AFTRA)
www.aftra.org

AFTRA is a national labor union representing nearly 80,000 artists in the entertainment and news media. Its sound recording membership includes classical artists and covers CDs, singles, Broadway cast albums, and audio books.

American Guild of Musical Artists (AGMA)
www.musicalartists.org

AGMA is a labor union that represents the men and women who create America's operatic, choral, and dance heritage.

RESOURCE

TIPS FOR A SUCCESSFUL RECORDING SESSION

Recording sessions are an exciting experience for singers, yet sessions often involve several hours of singing. Each piece may be performed three or four times to ensure proper coverage for final editing.

The following tips will help you prepare for a more rewarding and efficient recording experience.

1. Get plenty of sleep the night before the session. You will need "fresh ears" for the session.
2. Be sure your music is thoroughly polished and that you come to the session fully prepared. Technology is wonderful, but it cannot make up for a bad recording.
3. Do a thorough vocal warm-up before leaving for the recording session.
4. Time is money in a recording studio. The clock starts at the scheduled time whether you are there or not. Allow plenty of travel time for traffic, parking, and to locate the warm-up area. The warm-up area may or may not be located in the recording space.
5. Wear loose, comfortable clothes and shoes to the session, as you may have to be on your feet a lot. Studios are sometimes heavily air-conditioned, so bring a jacket or sweater with you to the session.
6. As with concert performances, do not wear perfumes, colognes, or other products that may irritate those around you. Do use deodorant, however.
7. Be sure to eat before the session. However, avoid foods that may affect your voice. See "The Care and Preservation of the Voice" in Chapter 7.
8. Bring a light snack for the break to maintain a high energy level during the session.
9. Room temperature water (not chilled) is best before a recording session.
10. Be sure to bring a pencil to the recording session.
11. Visit the restroom right before the session begins.
12. As you enter the recording area, take your assigned seat immediately. There will be a sound check at the beginning. The conductor may choose to move you to another seat. Be flexible.

13. An orchestra and/or soloists may be involved in the recording session. Pay attention, follow directions, and remain on top of things musically at all times. Be patient, for you may need to sit quietly as the soloists or orchestra perform additional takes of sections in the music.
14. The microphones will be very "hot." Turn pages quietly. Try not to sneeze or cough during a take. If coughing cannot be avoided, catch the eye of the conductor and leave the recording area quietly between takes. Do not call attention to yourself or disrupt the session.
15. Several seconds of complete silence are needed at the end of each take. Do not move or make a sound until the engineer indicates it is okay to do so.
16. If you make a mistake, do not let it get to you. Everyone makes mistakes in the recording studio. If you are upset by a mistake, it will affect the next take. Correct the mistake and move on.
17. The technical aspects of the music are incredibly important, but the emotion of the music must also come through on the recording.
18. Treat the producer, engineer, staff, conductor, your fellow singers, and yourself with respect.

RESOURCE

TRAVEL TIPS FOR SINGERS

Choir tours and out-of-town performances often provide singers with memories that last a lifetime. In addition, tours and run-out concerts (a concert held outside the primary performance venue) create a wonderful opportunity for the chorus members to bond as a group. Although personality conflicts may arise periodically, the experience with choir tours and run-out concerts is generally very positive.

Exploring other areas of the world, performing in musically historic venues, and learning about other cultures are often life-changing events for singers.

1. If the chorus is traveling out of the country, you will need a current passport. A visa may be required as well. As soon as you get information about the documentation you will need, obtain it immediately to avoid rushing right before you leave. There is a substantial price increase for expedited delivery of a passport. Your passport must be valid for at least six months beyond your return date from international destinations. Also, photocopies of your passport and visa will normally be requested from the tour company.
2. The U.S. State Department's website (http://travel.state.gov) has a wealth of information on other countries, including contact information for U.S. embassies and consulates, currency regulations, and safety/security warnings. Consular Information Sheets available on the site provide the entry requirements for every country. There is also information for foreign citizens who are planning to travel to the United States.
3. Make certain that your health insurance policy covers you while you are out of the country. Also, purchase travel insurance to protect you in case your baggage is lost, you have a medical emergency, or the trip is canceled. The small expense is worth it. The tour company will usually provide travel insurance information. If not, ask for it.
4. Meet with your doctor to discuss any medical needs or inoculations you should have prior to the departure date. A certificate will be required if you use syringes for medical reasons.

5. If you use prescription drugs, it is a good idea to carry an extra written prescription from your doctor in case the medication is lost or stolen during the trip. If any of your medications are restricted, you may also need to provide Customs with documentation from your doctor. Ask your doctor to write a letter on his or her letterhead listing all your prescription medications.

6. The tour company will usually provide a packing checklist. You should also monitor the weather of the cities on the tour so that you bring appropriate clothing. Depending on the tour destinations and time of year, you may encounter dramatic changes in climate. Be sure to pack clothing appropriate to the expected type of weather.

7. Pack sensibly. The tendency is to overdo it for a tour, especially for trips longer than a week. Pack only what you absolutely need. Carrying overloaded bags will be a chore, especially when the hotel is located at the top of a hill or incline. Also, some hotels do not have elevators.

8. Do not pack anything you are afraid of losing.

9. Be sure to attach a luggage tag with your name, address, and phone number to each piece of your luggage. Due to stricter airport security guidelines post–9/11, check with your airline regarding baggage restrictions, carry-ons, and forbidden items.

10. Plan your transportation to the airport—and make parking reservations, if needed—a few days in advance. For international travel, an earlier airport arrival will be required. Check ahead with your tour company or the airline.

11. Leave a copy of your travel itinerary with a family member or a friend so you can be reached in case of an emergency. Also leave a copy of your passport and visa at home, in case they are lost or stolen during the tour.

12. Get plenty of rest during the several days before the tour departure. Trying to make up for lost sleep while on the plane will leave you feeling even more fatigued.

13. Familiarize yourself with the exchange rate and currency of each country on the tour. Carry credit cards, debit cards, and traveler's checks rather than cash. Keep the receipts from your traveler's checks in a separate location. If the checks are lost or stolen during the trip, you can use the receipts to obtain replacements.

14. Purchase a telephone calling card to call home. Obtain the international and country access codes you will need.

15. Before leaving for the airport, do a final check to make sure you have the following:
    - Your passport and visa
    - A government-issued photo I.D., such as a driver's license
    - Your airline ticket
    - Every article of your concert attire
    - Your music and music folder
    - Traveler's checks, credit card, debit card, and a minimal amount of cash
    - Your glasses
    - Prescription medications and a medical certificate, if needed

16. A group check-in will usually take place at the airport. The tour director will do a head count to make sure all singers are present before boarding the plane.
17. If traveling by plane, set your watch to the time of your arrival city once you board to combat jet lag. Try to stay awake until the time that your final destination city would sleep.
18. Avoid excessive talking on an airplane, bus, or train. The noise level is high, so you have to speak loudly, which can result in vocal fatigue.
19. The air inside an airplane tends to be very dry. Drink as much water as possible. Keep your nasal passages moist by using saline nasal spray or antibacterial ointment.
20. Avoid alcohol and over-the-counter drugs such as antihistamines that cause dryness of the throat. One alcoholic beverage in the air equals two drinks on the ground.
21. Get up and move around the plane, bus, or train, and do some light stretching to avoid stiffness of the muscles and joints.
22. If it is daytime on arrival at the tour destination, try not to sleep until nighttime. Go outside and enjoy the sun. This will help your body clock adjust so that you adapt to the new time schedule much faster.
23. Keep your passport with you *at all times*.
24. Some meals, most often a continental breakfast, will be included in the tour cost. However, remember that food in other countries is not like the food at home. You will need to be open to new experiences food-wise.
25. The tour price generally includes the tip for the bus driver and tour escort.

RESOURCE

SUMMER CHORAL FESTIVALS

Each summer, a number of choral festivals take place across the country. Westminster Choir College (www.westminster.rider.edu) offers a summer choral festival for adults and a program for high school and middle school students.

Henry Leck, Founder and Artistic Director of the Indianapolis Children's Choir, serves each summer as the Artistic Director of the Pacific Rim Children's Chorus Festival (www.PacRimFestival.org). This nine-day residential program is designed for treble choirs in grades 6 through 12.

Children and youths may audition to be part of the World Youth Choir or World Children's Choir. These groups are made up of singers from more than 30 countries. For more information, visit the International Federation of Choral Music (IFCM) website at www.ifcm.net or www.worldyouthcholr.org.

The Berkshire Choral Festival (www.choralfest.org) provides singers with an opportunity to perform under the direction of renowned choral conductors. Most performances take place in Sheffield, Massachusetts. However, the Berkshire Choral Festival also provides singers with opportunities to perform in Canterbury, England, and Salzburg, Austria. In addition, the festival offers two scholarship programs for undergraduate and graduate students in music.

For more advanced singers, the Oregon Bach Festival (www.oregonbachfestival.com) affords participants the opportunity to sing under the direction of world-renowned conductor Helmut Rilling. Although a variety of literature is performed during the two-week festival, the music of J. S. Bach is the central focus. Singers are selected through competitive audition.

Summer choral festivals are a wonderful opportunity to perform with other singers across the country. The experience of singing and learning under the direction of a leading conductor expands the musical and vocal skills of choral singers. In turn, singers can apply their new skills to enhance their level of music making in their home chorus during the regular concert season.

R E S O U R C E

PROFESSIONAL SINGING OPPORTUNITIES

CHURCHES AND TEMPLES

Payment for professionals varies from organization to organization. Churches and temples tend to pay soloists a monthly stipend for services. As an example, the salary for a professional singer at a church may be $40 to $50 per rehearsal and the same amount per service. Some churches pay less, and some pay much more.

In addition to payment for regular services, additional income may be made by singing at weddings and funerals. The typical soloist fee may range from $100 to $150.

NONUNION PROFESSIONAL CHORUSES

Professional choruses not working under a union contract often pay singers a set fee for rehearsals and performances. The chorus may be made up entirely of professional singers or of volunteers with a professional core of singers.

Singers may earn $35 to $50 per rehearsal and $100 to $150 per performance in a non-union chorus.

UNION CONTRACTS

Choruses such as the San Francisco Symphony Chorus (www.sfsymphony.org) work under guidelines set forth by the American Guild of Musical Artists (AGMA) (www.musicalartists.org). AGMA is a labor union that represents artists in opera, choral music, and dance. The union negotiates with the company to set the amount of pay for each singer. For the 2003–2004 season of the San Francisco Symphony Chorus, professional singers were paid a minimum of $27.09 per rehearsal hour and $168.16 per performance.

Singers in the Los Angeles Opera Chorus were paid a minimum hourly rate of $35 and a performance fee of $146 for the 2003–2004 concert season. These amounts do not include additional payment for solos, transportation, meals, lodging, or overtime. Union contracts vary with each company. It is the singers' responsibility to familiarize themselves with the fine points of their contracts.

R E S O U R C E

FROM SINGER TO CONDUCTOR

Many of the world's finest singers performed in choruses at the start of their careers. For example, Marilyn Horne and Carol Neblett toured as members of the Roger Wagner Chorale. Although some choral singers choose to pursue solo careers, a small number of singers may choose to pursue a career as a choral conductor. And since choral conductors should possess experience as a singer or ensemble performer, the evolution from singer to conductor can be a very natural one.

Opportunities for choral conductors exist at all levels of the educational system, in churches, and with professional choirs and community choruses across the country. Some conductors come to the profession "by accident." Perhaps as the most talented singer in a church choir, they were asked to conduct a youth or children's chorus or to substitute for the director when he or she was out of town. Some choral singers fall in love with conducting immediately. In my own life, I knew from the beginning that choral conducting would be my career. I could not imagine pursuing anything else; choral music is my passion.

What are the characteristics of a successful choral conductor? Along with a thorough knowledge of the voice, the conductor must have an excellent ear. He or she must strive to be a great teacher who stimulates the imagination and musical creativity of the singers, inspiring the chorus to become a group of interdependent musicians who are relentless in their attention to detail.

As the leader of a chorus, a conductor must possess integrity, confidence, commitment, command of languages and the International Phonetic Alphabet (IPA), and the ability to work collaboratively with the singers, board of directors, administrators, and parents. The conductor must be an excellent communicator, an active leader in the community, and a creative problem-solver not only for administrative challenges but also to deal with the multitude of personalities that make up a chorus and music staff.

A successful conductor has a comprehensive knowledge of music history and style, musical score analysis, and orchestral instruments. He or she is disciplined yet creative and visionary and is ethical and passionate about music and making music with a group of singers.

GETTING STARTED

High school students who are planning to major in music in college will find that a thorough study of the basics of music will place them ahead of the game. Students who display exceptional knowledge of beginning theory and sight-reading skills may be placed in more advanced courses, often testing out of the beginning classes. See the "Music Theory, Sight-Reading, and Music History" section in Resource F: Online Choral Music Resources.

Opportunities exist for talented students to serve as the assistant to the conductor. Depending on your skills, you may be asked to lead a section rehearsal, warm up the choir, or conduct a piece during the concert. This type of experience is invaluable to young musicians. If opportunities such as these do not exist in your area, ask your high school choral teacher if he or she is willing to allow you to conduct a piece at your next concert. Perhaps the teacher will offer to teach you conducting or will point you in the direction of someone else who can.

Enroll in evening or summer classes in music theory and sight-reading at a local college. Learn about composers and listen to choral and instrumental music to expand your knowledge of literature. Piano classes can also prove to be invaluable. If you can accompany your future choirs, all the better. Early planning and preparation will set the stage for success when you audition for college music programs.

UNDERGRADUATE STUDY IN MUSIC

Students interested in becoming a choral conductor should consider entering an undergraduate program in music education with an emphasis in voice. A music education program allows students to develop their teaching skills in the classroom and become familiar with instruments in string, brass, and percussion classes while focusing on the voice as their main instrument. Conducting courses are included as part of the coursework for this degree as well.

Apply to undergraduate programs in schools with very strong master's and doctoral programs in choral conducting. This affords undergraduate students a better choral experience and education, many times with a leading authority in the field. In addition, students may elect to continue in the master's program once the bachelor of music degree has been completed.

There are many fine choral programs around the country. A list of the most prominent schools for choral conducting can be found on the ChoralNet website (www.choralnet.org) by clicking on "Education"; see entries under "College/ University Music Departments" in this section on the ChoralNet site. Luckily, most major colleges and universities now offer degrees in choral conducting at the master's and doctoral levels.

GRADUATE STUDY IN CHORAL CONDUCTING

Most colleges require at least two years of teaching experience prior to admitting a student into a master's program in choral conducting; for doctoral programs, the requirement is three or more years. Conducting positions have become quite competitive due to the number of colleges and universities offering degrees in choral conducting. Therefore, it has become difficult to place students in jobs without teaching experience.

Early exposure to choral music, theory, sight-reading, and musical style gives the budding conductor an advantage over the competition. Although you need a degree to get the interview, impressive skills and knowledge are what will ultimately convince an employer to hire you.

A BRIEF OVERVIEW OF CHORAL MUSIC HISTORY AND STYLE

MEDIEVAL PERIOD (CA. 400–1450)

General Period Characteristics
1. The church is the central figure in the development of music until about 1100. The church supports a majority of the composers of this period.
2. Secular music exists outside the church, made popular by traveling singers.
3. The birth of notation creates a body of music that, before this time, was passed down only by oral tradition.

Medieval Choirs: Made up of men and boys
Sound Ideal: Bright and forward, legato, vibrato used as an ornament only. The vocal tone should lighten when ascending and become more sonorous in the lower range.
Vocal Music Forms: Chanson, chant, madrigal, mass, motet, organum
Musical Texture: Monophonic. Polyphony emerged at the end of the medieval period.
Meter and Stress: Not metered; determined by the text
Tonality: Modal
Composers: Gilles Binchois (transitional to Renaissance), Hildegard von Bingen, Jacopa da Bologna, Guillaume Dufay (transitional to Renaissance), John Dunstable, Adam de la Halle, Leonin, Guillaume de Machaut, Perotin, Philippe de Vitry

Major Historical Events

Ca. 1150	The Cathedral of Notre Dame is built in Paris.
1338–1453	The Hundred Years' War takes place.
1348–1350	The Black Plague spreads.
1387	Chaucer begins writing *Canterbury Tales*.

Major Musical Events

590–604	Pope Gregory collects and codifies chant and organizes the *schola cantorum* or singing schools.
1025	Guido D'Arezzo develops a system of music notation. His system of music reading is the basis of our modern solfège system.

RENAISSANCE PERIOD (1450–1600)

General Period Characteristics
1. The term *Renaissance* means rebirth or awakening.
2. Secular music becomes more prominent.
3. Humanism emerges in Italy.
4. There is a change in the way the earth and universe are viewed.
5. There is renewed attention to philosophy, literature, and art of ancient Greece and Italy, Rome in particular.
6. Travel and musical exchange create a more international style in music.
7. Dynamic contrasts occur between sections of music and are dependent on changes in text or mood.
8. Dissonance and chromaticism are kept under strict control.
9. There is an increased patronage of music by religious institutions, rich courts, and civic governments.
10. Music printing allows more access to music and books about music.
11. Mature instrumental pieces appear.
12. Antiphonal writing for one or more choirs with brass and organ (polychoral style) becomes a musical feature of the late Renaissance.

Renaissance Choirs: Made up of men and boys. Male falsettists (*voci naturali*) sometimes double the boys. At times, castrati (referred to as *sopranisti* to distinguish them from the falsettists) sing the soprano or alto part with, or in lieu of, boys.
Sound Ideal: Bright and forward, light, legato, minimal vibrato
Vocal Music Forms: Anthem, carol, chanson, chorale, lieder, madrigal, mass, motet, psalm settings, villancico
Musical Texture: A contrast of homophonic (chordal) style with polyphonic sections. Frequent use of imitation. Four-part texture is standard and the vocal parts become more equal.
Meter and Stress: Determined by the text. Bar lines are developed near the end of the Renaissance, but are used only as a guide for the singers.
Tonality: Primarily modal. The concept of tonality through the use of more complete triads comes into being in the Renaissance.
Composers: Gilles Binchois, William Byrd, Giulio Caccini, Pierre Certon, Pierre de la Rue, Cristóbal de Morales, Josquin des Prés, John Dowland, Guillaume Dufay, John Farmer, Andrea Gabrieli, Giovanni Gabrieli (transitional to baroque), Jacobus Gallus, Carlo Gesualdo, Orlando Gibbons, Hans Leo Hassler (transitional to baroque), Heinrich Isaac, Clément Janequin, Orlando di Lasso, Luca Marenzio, Claudio Monteverdi (transitional to baroque), Thomas Morley, Jacob Obrecht, Johannes Okeghem, Giovanni Pierluigi da

Palestrina, Claudin de Sermisy, Thomas Tallis, John Taverner, Thomas Tomkins (transitional to baroque), Christopher Tye, Ludovico da Viadana (transitional to baroque), Tomás Luis de Vittoria, Thomas Weelkes (transitional to baroque), Giaches de Wert, Adrian Willaert

Major Historical Events

Ca. 1400	Humanism emerges in Italy.
1450	Johannes Gutenberg invents the printing press.
1452	Leonardo da Vinci is born.
1492	Columbus discovers North America.
1508–1512	Michelangelo paints the ceiling of the Sistine Chapel.
1517	Martin Luther begins the Protestant Reformation.
1519–1522	Ferdinand Magellan leads the first expedition to circumnavigate the globe.
1543	Copernicus completes his treatise on the new astronomy, explaining the relationship of the earth and sun.
1564	William Shakespeare is born.

Major Musical Events

1498	Ottaviano de Petrucci is granted the first license to print music, marking the beginning of music publishing.
1525	The greatest composer of Renaissance sacred music and leading composer of the Roman school, Giovanni Pierluigi da Palestrina, is born.
1555	Giovanni Gabrieli, the leading composer of the Venetian school of polychoral music, is born.

BAROQUE PERIOD (1600–1750)

General Period Characteristics
1. The baroque period sees an increasing importance in scientific observation and experimentation.
2. *Basso continuo* style emerges.
3. The *Doctrine of Affections*, a belief that music represented the feelings or moods of the text, arises during this period.

4. Terraced dynamics, dynamic changes occurring between sections of music, is a feature of baroque music.
5. Composers use dissonance and chromaticism to express the text.
6. Opera becomes an important source of entertainment.
7. The solo style develops.
8. Distinct styles of vocal and instrumental music develop in Italy, France, and Germany.
9. The violin becomes the most important string instrument. Virtuoso players such as Antonio Vivaldi and Archangelo Corelli represent this style in their compositions.
10. Instrumental forms develop to include the concerto and sonata.
11. Instruments accompany voices, often playing an equal role with the voices.
12. Some vocal music tends to be instrumentally conceived.
13. Castrati dominate serious opera.

Baroque Choirs: Made up of men and boys. Falsettists and castrati are still used in churches to reinforce the higher voice parts.
Sound Ideal: Light, agile, bright, bel canto, clear
Vocal Music Forms: Anthem, cantata, madrigal, magnificat, mass, motet, oratorio, passion, stabat mater, Te Deum, vespers
Musical Texture: Homophonic, polyphonic. Soloists are used to contrast larger choral forces.
Meter and Stress: Bar lines and metered music emerge during the baroque. However, the natural stress of the text should be given special attention rather than allowing for mechanical stresses to occur following the bar line.
Tonality: Major and minor tonalities become prominent.
Composers: Johann Sebastian Bach, John Blow, Dietrich Buxtehude, Giacomo Carissimi, Marc-Antoine Charpentier, Elisabeth-Claude Jacquet de la Guerre, Michel-Richard de Lalande, Giovanni Gabrieli, Andreas Hammerschmidt, George Frederic Handel, Hans Leo Hassler, Pelham Humfrey, Jean-Baptiste Lully, Claudio Monteverdi, Johann Pachelbel, Michael Praetorius, Henry Purcell, Alessandro Scarlatti, Samuel Scheidt, Johann Hermann Schein, Heinrich Schütz, Jan Pieterszoon Sweelinck, Georg Philip Telemann, Thomas Tomkins, Franz Tunder, Ludovico da Viadana, Antonio Vivaldi, Thomas Weelkes, Charles Wesley (transitional to classical)

Major Historical Events

1606	Rembrandt is born.
1607–1750	America is colonized.
1618	The Thirty Years' War begins.
1620	The Pilgrims arrive at Plymouth Rock on the *Mayflower*.
1666	Sir Isaac Newton discovers the law of gravity.

Major Musical Events

1600	Jacopo Peri's *Euridice* is the earliest surviving opera.
1685	J. S. Bach and Handel are born.
1709	Bartolomeo Cristofori invents the piano.
1742	Handel's *Messiah* is performed in Dublin.
1750	J. S. Bach dies.

CLASSICAL PERIOD (1750–1825)

General Period Characteristics

1. The center of cultural life is the palace, with Austria and Germany serving as musical centers of activity.
2. The church no longer dominates society.
3. Patrons, including royal courts, employ composers.
4. The classical period marks the beginning of public concerts with admission fees.
5. A variety of tempi are used during this period.
6. The Age of Enlightenment serves as a revolt against supernatural religion and emphasizes individual happiness.
7. Instrumental forms advance, with composers writing for orchestra, chamber orchestra, and solo instruments with orchestra.
8. The Industrial Revolution leads to an increase of goods and wealth.

Classical Choirs: Women join men and boys as part of the chorus. As larger works developed, the size of the chorus grows.
Sound Ideal: Light, agile, natural vibrato, flexible
Vocal Music Forms: Mass, missa brevis, opera choruses, oratorio, part songs, requiem mass, symphonic choral literature
Musical Texture: Homophonic texture becomes the standard.
Meter and Stress: Classical music uses simpler rhythm patterns. In general, music dominates the text.
Tonality: Major and minor. Harmonies are simpler and more predictable.
Composers: Ludwig van Beethoven, William Billings, Luigi Cherubini (transitional to romantic), Franz Joseph Haydn, Michael Haydn, Wolfgang Amadeus Mozart, Charles Wesley, Samuel Wesley (transitional to romantic)

Major Historical Events

1752	Benjamin Franklin discovers electricity.
1776	The Declaration of Independence of the Thirteen Colonies is signed.
1789	The French Revolution begins.

Major Musical Events

1791	Mozart begins composing the *Requiem*, but dies before it is completed.
1798	Haydn's *Creation* is performed in Vienna.
1807	Beethoven composes the *Fifth Symphony*.
1814	Maelzel patents the metronome.

ROMANTIC PERIOD (1825–1900)

General Period Characteristics

1. The main audience for the composer is the concert-going public rather than clergy or royalty.
2. A vocabulary of expressive musical terms develops during the romantic period.
3. There is a revolt against classical rules and traditions. The romantic composers expand classical form and make them more expressive.
4. Romantic composers are inspired by nature, fantasy, the supernatural, and literature.
5. The musician is viewed as an artist. Music is viewed as a calling rather than an occupation.
6. Composers use music as a vehicle for emphasizing national identity.
7. Dynamics ranging from *ppp* to *fff* are used during this period.
8. Crescendo and decrescendo become widely used.
9. The orchestra becomes larger. Instruments are mass produced, making them cheaper and more available.
10. The art song for solo voice with piano accompaniment emerges during the romantic period.
11. Music conservatories replace the apprentice system. Musicians with better training provide composers with the talent necessary to perform their works.

Romantic Choirs: Choral singing becomes an important activity in larger cities in Europe and America. The size of the chorus is greatly expanded for performances with orchestras.

Sound Ideal: Rich, warm, round, supple, and soloistic
Vocal Music Forms: Cantata, folk songs, mass, opera choruses, oratorio, part songs, requiem mass, symphonic choral literature
Musical Texture: Somewhat dense and heavy. Melodies become longer and harmonies fuller, often employing dissonance.
Meter and Stress: Composers seek to break the strictness of rhythm through metric alteration and extended or irregular phrases.
Tonality: Major and minor tonality is still dominant, yet composers begin to experiment with other harmonic ideas to express the emotion of the music.
Composers: Amy Beach (transitional to modern), Hector Berlioz, Johannes Brahms, Anton Bruckner, Luigi Cherubini, Antonin Dvorák, Sir Edward Elgar (transitional to modern), Gabriel Fauré (transitional to modern), Stephen Foster, Fanny Mendelssohn Hensel, Leoš Janáček (transitional to modern), Franz Liszt, Gustav Mahler, Felix Mendelssohn, Horatio Parker (transitional to modern), Max Reger (transitional to modern), Joseph Rheinberger, Gioacchino Rossini, Camille Saint-Saëns, Robert Schumann, Franz Schubert, Giuseppi Verdi, Richard Wagner, Hugo Wolf

Major Historical Events

1821	The electric motor and generator are invented.
1840	The first electric light bulb is invented.
1848	The California Gold Rush begins.
1859	Charles Darwin writes *Origin of the Species*.
1861	The Civil War begins in America.
1863	Lincoln gives the Gettysburg Address; Emancipation Proclamation is delivered.
1865	Lincoln is assassinated; slavery is outlawed.
1876	Bell invents the telephone.
1877	Edison invents the phonograph.

Major Musical Events

1827	Beethoven dies.
1837	Berlioz composes the *Grandes Messe des Morts*.
1847	Mendelssohn's *Elijah* is first performed in Birmingham, England.
1868	Brahms completes the *German Requiem*.
1874	Verdi composes the *Manzoni Requiem*.

MODERN MUSIC (1900-PRESENT)

General Period Characteristics
1. Technology and science advance at a phenomenal rate.
2. The radio and phonograph make music accessible to millions of people.
3. Popular music, especially jazz, country, and rock, becomes a central focus, especially in the last half of the 20th century.
4. The advent of sound recording changes the way people listen to music.
5. Composers become more and more interested in the music of other cultures.
6. Books about choral music are published.
7. National music organizations are formed.
8. Composers use nontraditional scale patterns.
9. There is a preference for more percussive effects in music.
10. Most universities and colleges have degree programs in music.

Modern Choirs: Due to significant developments and opportunities in choral music education, singers of all ages and voice types perform in choruses. Professional choirs such as the Robert Shaw Chorale and Roger Wagner Chorale toured and recorded extensively.
Sound Ideal: Depending on the style of music, the tone quality of the singer will vary from light and delicate to dark and powerful in electronic and world music.
Vocal Music Forms: Cantata, choral pieces accompanied by chamber orchestra, mass, missa brevis, musical theatre, opera choruses, oratorio, popular music, psalm settings, requiem, spiritual, symphonic choral literature, Te Deum
Musical Texture: Chordal to contrapuntal. Melodies become more angular and contain wider intervals.
Meter and Stress: Rhythm becomes more complex, constant changes in meter become the norm. Less tension and rhythmic drive occur in Impressionistic music.
Tonality: Major, minor, atonal, modal, based on nontraditional scales such as the whole tone or pentatonic scale. Composers explore bitonality and polytonality, two or more key centers at the same time.
Composers: Domenick Argento, Henk Badings, Samuel Barber, Béla Bartók, Amy Beach, Leonard Bernstein, Benjamin Britten, Pablo Casals, David Conte, Aaron Copland, John Corigliano, Claude Debussy, Norman Dello Joio, Hugo Distler, Maurice Duruflé, Sir Edward Elgar, Gabriel Fauré, Irving Fine, Lukas Foss, George Gershwin, Henryk Górecki, Paul Hindemith, Gustav Holst, Arthur Honegger, Herbert Howells, Charles Ives, Leoš Janáček, Zoltán Kodály, Morten Lauridsen, Györgi Ligeti, Frank Martin, Gian Carlo Menotti, James Mulholland, John Jacob Niles, Carl Orff, Alice Parker, Horatio Parker, Arvo Pärt, Stephen Paulus, Krzysztof Penderecki, Vincent Persichetti, Craig Phillips, Daniel Pinkham, Francis Poulenc, Sergei Prokofiev, Sergei Rachmaninoff, Maurice Ravel, Max Reger, Ned Rorem,

Arnold Schönberg, William Schuman, Stephen Sondheim, Sir Charles Villiers Stanford, Igor Stravinsky, Conrad Susa, Karol Szymanowski, Randall Thompson, Ralph Vaughan Williams, Heitor Villa-Lobos, Sir William Walton, Eric Whitacre, Healey Willan

Major Historical Events

1903	The Wright brothers complete their first successful airplane flight.
1905	Albert Einstein introduces the theory of relativity.
1912	The *Titanic* sinks.
1914–1918	World War I is fought across Europe.
1939	World War II begins.
1941	Pearl Harbor is attacked; United States enters World War II.
1945	The first atomic bomb is dropped; World War II ends.
1957	The first satellite is launched.
1961	First man goes into space.
1963	President John F. Kennedy is assassinated.
1969	First man lands and walks on the moon.
1979	Iranian hostage crisis occurs.
1989	The Berlin Wall falls.
2001	The World Trade Center is destroyed by terrorists.

Major Musical Events

1924	The Juilliard School opens in New York.
1930	Stravinsky completes *Symphony of Psalms*.
1935–1936	Carl Orff composes *Carmina Burana*.
1945	Britten's *Peter Grimes* premiers in London, marking the rebirth of British opera.
1957	Leonard Bernstein completes *West Side Story*.
1959	The first Grammy Award ceremony takes place.
1969	Woodstock Music Festival occurs.
1976	Philip Glass completes the first widely known example of minimalist music, *Einstein on the Beach*.
1988	CDs begin to outsell vinyl records.
1992	Roger Wagner dies.
1999	Robert Shaw dies.

A

absolute pitch The ability to instantaneously identify pitch without an external reference. Also referred to as *perfect pitch*.

a cappella Literally, "in chapel style"; music performed without accompaniment.

accent A symbol placed above or below a note or chord indicating stress or emphasis.

acciaccatura Meaning "crushed" in Italian, this symbol is notated with the stem of the note crossed through and is performed as quickly as possible on the beat.

accidental A flat, sharp, or natural in a bar of music that is not included as part of the original key signature. The accidental is valid only for the bar in which it appears.

acoustics The study of the physical properties of sound; the reflection of sound and resonance in a concert hall or rehearsal room.

agogic accent Accentuation of a note through longer duration rather than singing it forcefully.

alto Meaning "high" in Italian, the voice part below the **soprano**, which may be sung by women, men, or children. Also called *contralto*.

anacrusis See **upbeat**.

anthem An English choral composition sung at a religious service. Comparable to the **motet** in the Roman Catholic liturgy.

antiphony A style of singing using alternating choirs.

appoggiatura From the Italian "to lean," the *appoggiatura* is a nonharmonic tone, which "leans" into the main note on the beat and halves its time.

aria A composition written for a solo vocalist with instrumental accompaniment; found in cantatas, operas, and oratorios.

arpeggio Literally "in the manner of a harp," a chord performed with the notes "spread out." The notes are not sounded simultaneously, but in succession from bottom to top.

arsis-thesis Lifting and lowering; building to a climax of tension in a phrase and relaxing to the resolution.

articulation The action of the speech organs in the formation of vowels, consonants, syllables, and words. To a singer or instrumentalist, articulation also refers to the execution of interpretive elements such as accents, legato, marcato, and staccato.

art song A self-contained composition for voice and piano, intended to be presented as a work of art.

atonality The absence of **tonality**; not in any key.

attack The onset of sound.

augmentation A restatement of a melody in a composition in longer note values; the opposite of **diminution**.

augmented A major or perfect interval, or the fifth of a triad that has been enlarged (augmented) by one-half step (e.g., c–g, a perfect fifth, becomes an augmented fifth by raising the note G to g-sharp; likewise, the major triad c–e–g becomes an augmented triad by raising the G to a g-sharp). Augmented intervals or triads, like majors, are notated using capital letters (e.g., *A5* for an augmented fifth or *Aug.* to indicate an augmented triad, as in *CAug.*).

B

bar A metrical division of music into one measure.

baritone The male voice with a range between **tenor** and **bass**.

bar line A vertical line on the staff that divides music into measures.

baroque period Following the Renaissance, the period of musical style between 1600 and 1750.

bass The lowest male voice; the lowest parts in a musical composition.

bass clef 𝄢 Also called the *F clef*, the bass clef is a sign placed at the beginning of the staff to indicate that the fourth line up on the staff is the note F below middle C. The two dots of this clef surround the line for the note F on the staff.

basso continuo Employed most often in the baroque period, *basso continuo* (also referred to as *continuo* or *thoroughbass*) is an ensemble of at least two instruments—a harmonic instrument, such as an organ or a harpsichord, and a bass instrument such as a viola da gamba, a cello, or a bassoon—in performance. The harmonic instrument plays the written-out bass line and melody, filling in the chords with the help of figures (numerals indicating chords) written below the bass line to indicate harmonies, as the bass instrument reinforces the bass line.

basso ostinato See **ostinato**.

beat A regularly recurring pulse that divides time into equal segments. See also **tactus**.

bel canto Italian for "beautiful singing," *bel canto* refers to an 18th-century Italian vocal technique that emphasized beautiful sound and virtuosic performance.

binary form A musical work in two sections, popular in the dances of the baroque period.

blend The combination of pitch accuracy, rhythmic accuracy, and vowel unification in choral performance.

bridge A short section of a composition that links together two sections of the work. Also called *transition*.

broken chord A chord in which notes are played one after the other, rather than at the same time.

C

cadence A progression of chords that gives the effect of ending a "sentence" in music.

cadenza A florid solo passage near the end of a work to display the virtuosity of a singer or player and encourage applause. *Cadenzas* were improvised traditionally, but today they are generally written out by performers.

cambiata A boy's changing voice.

canon A melody repeated in full by another voice or instrument. The second voice begins before the first voice has finished, which causes overlapping. The best-known form of a canon is the *round*, or perpetual canon, where each voice begins again after it finishes the melody. Familiar examples of the round are the songs "Row, Row, Row Your Boat" and "Three Blind Mice."

cantata A baroque sacred or secular choral composition, usually with instrumental accompaniment, consisting of a number of movements containing solos, duets, arias, recitatives, and choruses.

canticle A song, hymn, or chant with a religious text, other than from the Psalms, used in church liturgy; a concert work with a religious text.

cantor The person who leads the singing in a religious service; also refers to the director of music in the early Protestant church. J. S. Bach was the cantor at St. Thomas in Leipzig, for example. Alternate spelling is *kantor*.

cantus firmus Fixed melody; a preexisting melody, usually based on **Gregorian chant**, used as the basis for a polyphonic composition to which other parts are added.

carol A traditional song of joyful character, usually for the celebration of Christmas.

chanson French for "song," a type of lyrical polyphonic music, sometimes with instruments, for several voices. The *chanson* was popular in France in the 15th and 16th centuries.

chant Monophonic, unaccompanied liturgical music in free rhythm and containing a limited vocal range.

chantey A song sung by English and American sailors in rhythm with their work; alternative spellings are *chanty* and *shanty*.

chanty See **chantey**.

chest voice The lowest range of the voice in singing or speaking.

choir A group of singers most often connected to a church or religious institution. Also describes the part of the church where the singers are to be seated.

chorale A hymn tune of the German Protestant Church characterized by block chords. Chorales are a prominent feature of the German Passion oratorio.

choral music Music written for chorus or choir; vocal music, with or without instrumental accompaniment, for more than one singer on a part.

choral symphony A symphonic work written for voices; the popular name for Beethoven's *Ninth Symphony*.

chord Generally the combination of three or more notes sounded together.

chorister A choir singer; a boy singer in an English choir.

chorus A group of singers not connected with a church or religious institution; a group of people assembled to sing together. The refrain of a song is also referred to as the chorus.

chromatic Ascending or descending by half steps; from the Greek meaning "colored."

chromatic scale The scale made up of all the half steps within an octave.

classical period Following the baroque period, the period of musical style roughly between 1750 and 1825.

clef A sign placed at the beginning of the staff, indicating the pitch of the notes on the staff. The most common clefs are the *treble*, or *G clef*, and the *bass*, or *F clef*.

coloratura A florid style of vocal music requiring a solid vocal technique to execute rapid passages, trills, or runs. The "Queen of the Night" aria from *The Magic Flute* is a familiar example.

coloratura soprano The highest female voice, specializing in coloratura singing.

common time Another name for 4/4 time, or 4 quarter notes to the bar.

concert A musical performance, usually with several performers, in front of an audience.

concertato The alternation of a small group of singers or instrumentalists to contrast the full chorus or orchestra, especially common in the music of the baroque period.

concertmaster The first violin in an orchestra, placed right next to the conductor's podium. The concertmaster leads the orchestra in its tuning prior to the concert, customarily plays all of the violin solos, and determines the appropriate bowings so that all the violinists are bowing in unison.

conductor The person who conducts the choir or orchestra in rehearsal and performance.

consonance A smooth- or agreeable-sounding interval; the opposite of **dissonance**. The consonant intervals are unisons, thirds, fourths, fifths, and octaves.

contralto See **alto**.

coperta A "covered" sound, yet brilliant and balanced from top to bottom throughout the range.

cori spezzati Divided choirs of the Venetian polychoral style. Choirs were placed in various parts of the church to create a spatial effect.

countertenor A rare male voice higher than a **tenor**; a male **alto**.

crescendo (cresc.) ———— A gradual increase in volume.

D

decrescendo (decr. or decres.) ———— A gradual decrease in volume; same as *diminuendo*.

descant An **obbligato** melody that soars above the given melody, adding interest to the final verse of a hymn or carol.

diaphragm A thin, dome-shaped sheet of muscle situated below the lungs and heart that separates the chest cavity from the abdomen; the main muscle of inspiration.

diatonic A major or minor scale of eight notes; tones in music that are confined to notes in the key, excluding chromatic tones.

diction The combination of **pronunciation**, **enunciation**, and **articulation** in singing.

diminished A perfect or minor interval that has been lowered (diminished) by one-half step (e.g., c–g, a perfect fifth, becomes a diminished fifth by lowering the note G to g-flat). Diminished intervals or triads, like minors, are notated using lowercase letters (e.g., *d5* for a diminished fifth or *dim* to indicate a diminished triad, e.g., *cdim*).

diminuendo (dim.) See **decrescendo**.

diminution A restatement of a melody in a composition with decreasing (usually half) note values from the original melody; the opposite of **augmentation**.

diphthong Two vowel sounds in succession (e.g., the *ah* and *ih* sounds made in saying the word *night*).

dissonance Interval sounds of unrest or discord; the opposite of **consonance**. The dissonant intervals are seconds, sevenths, and the tritone.

do In solfeggio, the first degree of a major scale.

dominant The fifth scale degree, or a chord built on the fifth degree of the scale.

dot A rhythmic notational symbol placed after a note, indicating that the note should be extended by half its original value. A double dot placed after a note extends the time by three-quarters of the original value of the note.

double bar A pair of vertical lines on that staff indicating the end of a section or composition.

double flat ♭♭ Two flat signs before a note that lowers the note two half steps (one whole step).

double sharp × A sign, like an x, before a note that raises the note two half steps (one whole step).

downbeat The downward motion of the conductor's hand or baton, which indicates the strong beats in a bar of music; the first beat of a measure.

drone A continuous sound on one or more fixed pitches.

duet A performance by two singers or instrumentalists of a composition containing two parts of equal importance.

duple meter Music with two beats per measure. The most common examples are 2/2, 2/4, 2/8, and 6/8.

dynamics The loudness or softness of a tone.

E

early music European music of the medieval, Renaissance, and baroque periods.

eighth note ♪ A note which is equal to one-half the value of a quarter note.

encore Meaning "again" in French, applause from the audience demanding an additional or repeated performance of a piece; an extra piece performed at the end of a performance.

enharmonic A term used to describe two notes that sound the same but are spelled differently (e.g., c-sharp and d-flat).

ensemble Meaning "together" in French, a group of performers who regularly play or sing together. The term is also used to describe the quality of teamwork present in the performance.

enunciation Making a song's lyrics intelligible through the fullness and clarity of the sound, resulting in ease of perception by the listener.

epiglottis A thin, leaf-shaped cartilage situated at the back of the tongue, which covers the vocal folds to prevent food or liquid from entering the **trachea** (and lungs) during swallowing.

esophagus The food tube situated behind the **trachea**, which connects the mouth to the stomach.

F

fa In solfeggio, the fourth degree of a major scale.

falsettist See **falsetto**.

falsetto The "false" voice of a male singer that allows him to produce pitches beyond his normal range. Also, a singer who uses falsetto; also called a *falsettist*.

F clef See **bass clef**.

fixed do The note C is always *do*, regardless of the key. Compare with **movable do**.

flat A symbol ♭ that lowers the pitch of a note by one-half step. This term is also used to describe a singer or instrumentalist who plays or sings below the true pitch.

folk music Generally, music passed down through aural tradition within a community, making it subject to modification when it is written down.

form The structure or design of a piece of music. The **fugue** is an example of a basic form in music.

forte Abbreviated as *f*, an instruction for the singer or instrumentalist to perform at a loud dynamic level.

fortissimo Abbreviated as *ff*, an instruction for the singer or instrumentalist to perform at a very loud dynamic level.

fugue Meaning "flight," the *fugue* is a polyphonic compositional technique in which the composer introduces a musical theme (melody) that is imitated at a higher or lower pitch by the other voices. Johann Sebastian Bach composed many of the greatest fugues.

fundamental The primary note (lowest tone) of the overtone series.

G

G clef See **treble clef**.

glee club A club, either male or female, organized to sing together.

glide A pitched consonant that has the sound of a vowel (e.g., *w* and *y*); also called a *semivowel* or *semiconsonant*.

glissando A musical effect caused by rapid "sliding" between two pitches.

glottal attack A "pop" produced by excessive tension in the closure of the vocal cords at the onset of sound.

glottis The V-shaped airspace between the vocal cords.

grace note An ornament, written as a small note, to the main melody. The grace note takes its time away from the note it is attached to and is performed rapidly just before the beat.

grand staff Two staves with the treble and bass clefs connected by a brace.

Gregorian chant Often referred to as Roman chant, plainsong, or plainchant, Gregorian chant is the liturgical chant of the Roman Catholic Church. It was systemized by Pope Gregory (590–604), hence the name "Gregorian."

ground bass The English term for *basso ostinato*. See **ostinato**.

H

half note ♩ A note that is one-half the value of a whole note and twice the value of a quarter note.

half step An interval, ascending or descending, from one pitch to the nearest adjacent pitch on the piano keyboard; the smallest interval on the keyboard. (e.g., c–c-sharp); also referred to as a *semitone*.

hard palate The bony part of the roof of the mouth, which sits in front of the soft palate.

harmonic minor scale A form of the minor scale using an accidental to raise the seventh degree by one-half step, producing a leading tone between the seventh and eighth scale degrees. The pattern for a harmonic minor scale is 1–1/2–1–1–1/2–1 1/2–1/2 (e.g., a harmonic minor scale built on the note C is c–d–e-flat–f–g–a-flat–b–c).

harmonics See **overtones**.

harmony The simultaneous sounding of notes, representing the vertical aspect of music.

head voice The highest range of the voice in singing.

homophonic Having voices or instruments move together in a chordal fashion; the opposite of **polyphonic**

hymn Traditionally a song of praise to a god or hero, today hymns are Christian songs that are sung by a church congregation.

I

ictus From the Latin for "strike," the *ictus* represents the point of each beat in the conductor's gesture, which communicates the pulse of the tempo to the singers or instrumentalists.

imitation The exact duplication, sometimes on a different pitch, of a melodic line in other voice parts.

impressionism A French movement of the late 19th and early 20th century conceived by Debussy in reaction to the dramatic emotionalism of romantic music, especially that of Wagner.

improvisation The spontaneous creation of music by a performer.

International Phonetic Alphabet (IPA) A system of symbols that provide a pronunciation key for all languages. The IPA was developed by British and French phoneticians and established in Paris in 1896 as a model to encourage uniformity in speaking and singing.

interval The distance in pitch between two tones.

intonation The extent to which the performers sing or play in tune. Intonation also refers to the opening tones of a chant sung by a cantor or priest.

K

kantor See **cantor**.

key The tonal center of the music. "Key" may also refer to a lever on an instrument such as a piano, which is pressed to produce sound.

key signature The flats or sharps placed at the beginning of each staff or at key changes to indicate the key of the composition.

L

la In solfeggio, the sixth degree of a major scale.

larynx The organ of voice production containing the vocal cords, situated at the top of the trachea (windpipe).

leading tone The seventh scale degree of a major, harmonic minor, or ascending melodic minor scale. The leading tone is one-half step below the tonic note and has a strong tendency to resolve upward toward the tonic.

ledger line A short horizontal line written above or below the five main lines of the staff to accommodate notes that lie outside the range of the staff.

legato Meaning "bound together" in Italian, *legato* is a direction for the singer to phrase in a smooth and connected manner without interruption between the notes; the opposite of **staccato**.

libretto Meaning "little book," the *libretto* is the text of an opera or oratorio. In the past, the libretto was distributed as a booklet to members of the audience.

lied (pl. **lieder**) The German word for "song," a *lied* is a song in the German vernacular, corresponding to the **chanson** in France. In the early 19th century, the lied evolved into a German art song for voice with piano accompaniment.

lift See **register change**.

litany A series of supplicant prayers to God, the Virgin, or the saints, usually with the congregation making a fixed response.

liturgy From the Latin meaning "the work of the people," *liturgy* refers to the structure of worship within the Christian church.

lyricist A person who writes the words, or lyrics, of a song.

lyrics The words of a song.

M

madrigal A secular song, usually on an amorous theme, for several voice parts, first popular in Italy during the 14th century and later revived in Italy and England in the 16th century.

Magnificat A canticle of the Virgin Mary in 12 verses, expressing her joy and thanksgiving for God's promise to redeem the world through the birth of her Son. The text is taken from Luke 1:46–55.

major The designation for certain intervals and scales. Major is notated using capital letters (e.g., C-Major or M3 to indicate a major third).

major scale A diatonic scale containing half steps between scale degrees 3 and 4 and 7 and 8. The other scale degrees are made up of whole steps. The key of the scale is determined by the first note, or tonic (e.g., a C-Major scale is c–d–e–f–g–a–b–c).

marcato A direction for the singer or instrumentalist to "mark" or emphasize a note or series of notes.

marking Singing without the full voice in rehearsal during sickness or prior to a performance to preserve the voice.

Mass The principal service of the Roman Catholic Church, commemorating the Last Supper of Christ. High Mass is sung, whereas Low Mass is spoken.

measure A bar of music.

mediant The third scale degree or a chord built upon the third scale degree.

medieval period The period of musical style (c. 400–1450) preceding the baroque, representing the music of the early Christian church; also referred to as the Middle Ages.

melisma A group of notes sung to a single syllable.

melodic minor scale A form of the minor scale using accidentals to raise the sixth and seventh degrees in the ascending form, creating half steps between scale degrees 2 and 3 and 7 and 8. The descending form of the scale does not use the accidentals, making it the same pattern as a natural minor scale. The ascending pattern of the melodic minor scale is 1–1/2–1–1–1–1–1/2. The descending pattern is 1–1–1/2–1–1–1/2–1 (e.g., a melodic minor scale built on C is c–d–e-flat–f–g–a–b–c in ascending form and c–b-flat–a-flat–g–f–e-flat–d–c in descending form).

melody A succession of musical tones that forms a recognizable musical shape. The melody represents the linear or horizontal aspect of music.

messa di voce A crescendo/decrescendo on a single, sustained tone.

meter A system of musical pulse, accented and unaccented, within a measure, indicated by the meter signature at beginning of the work.

meter signature Numbers placed at the beginning of a musical work showing the grouping of the beats and the value of the basic beat. The upper number indicates the number of beats in a measure, whereas the lower number indicates the note value of the beat. Also called *time signature*.

metronome Patented in 1814 by Maelzel, who purportedly stole the invention from D. N. Winkel, the metronome is used to sound an adjustable number of beats per minute to establish a consistent tempo. Metronome markings appear in the upper left-hand corner of the composition. M.M. ♩=60 refers to Maelzel's Metronome (M.M.) with 60 quarter-note beats in one minute.

mezzo forte Abbreviated as *mf*, an instruction for the singer or instrumentalist to perform at a moderately loud dynamic level.

mezzo piano Abbreviated as *mp*, an instruction for the singer or instrumentalist to perform at a moderately soft dynamic level.

mezzo-soprano A female voice with a range between **soprano** and **alto**.

mi In solfeggio, the third degree of a major scale.

middle voice A vocal sound having the qualities of both head and chest voice; the middle of the vocal range. Also called *mixed voice*.

minor The designation for certain intervals and scales. Minor is notated using lowercase letters (e.g., c-minor or m3 to indicate a minor third).

minor scale Any one of three diatonic scales: natural minor, harmonic minor, or melodic minor. The key of the scale is determined by the first note, or tonic.

Missa brevis A short Mass or a Lutheran Mass that consists of only the Kyrie and Gloria.

mixed voice See **middle voice**.

mixed voices A combination of male and female voices; SATB.

modulation A change from one key to another within a musical composition.

monophonic From the Greek meaning "single sound"; having a single, unaccompanied melody.

motet A sacred, unaccompanied choral composition performed in the Roman Catholic service. Comparable to the **anthem** in England.

movable do The note designated as *do* changes depending on the key of the music. *Do* is the first note, or tonic, of the key (e.g., in the key of C-Major, *do* = C). Compare with **fixed do**.

movement A self-contained section of a larger work.

music Derived from the Greek term *mousa*, meaning any of the nine sister goddesses, or Muses, who preside over the arts in Greek mythology, *music* is the organization of sounds and silences through time in an arrangement that pleases the ear. Music expresses ideas and emotions through melody, harmony, rhythm, and tone color.

music appreciation An introductory course in music and music listening, with the intention of increasing love, understanding, and appreciation for music throughout history.

music history The study of how music has evolved over time with regard to topics such as musical style and form, composers, notation, and musical instruments.

musicology The scholarly study of music and music history.

music theory The study, through analysis and composition, of the elements of music and how music is put together.

N

nasopharynx The area of the throat behind the nose and above the soft palate.

natural ♮   A musical symbol that cancels a previous sharp or flat. Natural also refers to a note that is neither sharp nor flat (e.g., c-natural).

natural minor scale Also referred to as pure minor, the natural minor scale is a form of the minor scale containing half steps between scale degrees 2 and 3 and 5 and 6. Thus, a natural minor scale built on the note A is a–b–c–d–e–f–g–a.

neutral syllable A syllable used for sight-reading new music.

neutral vowel See **schwa**.

nonharmonic tone A note (or notes) that are not part of the triad or chord with which it sounds.

notation A system of symbols used to create a musical composition.

note A single sound of a particular pitch and length.

O

obbligato From the Italian for "obligatory," *obbligato* refers to the obligatory use of an instrument in a musical work; a melody of some independence that accompanies another musical idea.

octave The interval of eight notes above a given pitch. An octave above the given pitch contains twice the vibrations per second as the original pitch; the octave below the given pitch contains half the vibrations per second.

octet A composition for, or a group of, eight singers or instrumentalists.

opera A dramatic, staged work with costumes and elaborate sets comprising an overture, recitatives, arias, and choruses with orchestral accompaniment.

opera chorus A group of singers assembled to perform the choruses in an opera; also, a chorus from an opera.

opus (pl. **opera**) From the Latin meaning "work"; composers generally catalogue their compositions in chronological order using opus numbers (e.g., Op. 1).

oratorio A large-scale sacred work without staging, costumes, or scenery, comprising an overture, recitatives, arias, and choruses with orchestral accompaniment. Oratorios were performed outside the sanctuary in the *oratorium*, especially during the Lenten season when operas were not permitted to be performed.

Ordinary of the Mass The five sung portions of the Mass for which the texts do not vary. Its sections include the Kyrie, Gloria, Credo, Sanctus (Benedictus), and Agnus Dei.

ornament One or more notes added by the composer or performer to embellish a melody.

ostinato A repeated melodic or rhythm pattern, often appearing in the bass line. Also called *basso ostinato* or *ground bass*.

overtones Secondary pitches above or below the fundamental pitch that, when taken in sum, help form the totality of the sound. Also referred to as *harmonics* or *partials*.

overture An orchestral composition that introduces an opera, oratorio, or smaller work, usually alluding to what is to follow.

P

part An independent line or voice in a musical composition.

partials See **overtones**.

part song A choral composition written for several voice parts in homophonic style, particularly as it applies to music of 19th-century composers such as Haydn, Mendelssohn, and Schumann.

passaggio Italian for "passageway"; the transition from one register to another.

Passion A musical setting of the suffering and death of Jesus, as told by one of the four evangelists. The Passion is normally to be sung in the week before Easter and contains solos, recitatives, and choruses with instrumental accompaniment. Today, concert versions of the Passion are performed throughout the year.

pedal tone A long note, generally in the bass part, that is held while other voices move above it.

pentatonic scale A five-note scale, often represented by the black keys on the piano, used in folk music and non-Western music.

perfect pitch See **absolute pitch**.

pharynx The airway in the back of the throat between the **larynx** and behind the nose.

phonation The production of a vocal sound or the act of starting a sound.

phrase A musical "sentence" or a complete musical thought.

phrase marking A curved line over a series of notes, indicating that the singer or instrumentalist should connect, without a breath, all notes in the series.

pianissimo Abbreviated as *pp*, an instruction for the singer or instrumentalist to perform at a very soft dynamic level.

piano Abbreviated as *p*, an instruction for the singer or instrumentalist to perform at a soft dynamic level.

Picardy third (*Tierce de Picardie*) A raised third scale degree, making a major triad, in the final chord of a composition written in a minor key. This practice originated around 1500 and was common up to the mid-18th century.

pickup See **upbeat**.

pitch The highness or lowness of a tone.

polyphonic Meaning "many sounds," polyphonic texture involves two or more simultaneous musical lines moving independently of one another. The opposite of **homophonic**.

portamento A smooth vocal or instrumental slide from one note to another without interruption; often employed in opera.

portato A direction for the singer to articulate a note or series of notes halfway between legato and staccato. *Portato* is usually indicated by a slur with dots under or above each note.

pronunciation The manner in which a singer produces a word with regard to both sound color and syllable stress.

Proper of the Mass The five sections of the Mass sung to texts that vary depending on the liturgical season. Its sections include the Introit, Gradual, Alleluia-Verse (or Tract), Offertory, and Communion.

pulse A regularly recurring beat.

Q

quadruple meter Music with four beats per measure. The most common examples are 4/2, 4/4, 4/8, C (common time), and 12/8.

quarter note ♩ A note that is equivalent to one beat in 4/4 time.

quartet A composition for, or a group of, four singers or instrumentalists.

quintet A composition for, or a group of, five singers or instrumentalists.

R

range The gamut of pitches, from low to high, that a singer performs beautifully.

re In solfeggio, the second degree of a major scale.

recapitulation The return of previous material in a composition.

recital A musical performance, generally by one or two performers or several members of a vocal or instrumental studio, given in front of an audience.

recitative Generally preceding an aria or chorus in an opera, oratorio, or cantata, recitative is musically heightened speech characterized by free rhythm and clarity of text. The recitative reports dramatic action and helps to advance the plot.

refrain Part of a section of music that recurs at the end of each verse or stanza; some-times referred to as the *chorus*.

register A series of tones produced in a like manner at the level of the **larynx**.

register change The note at which the vocal tone changes abruptly; also called a *lift*.

relative pitch A musician's ability to identify intervals between a given note and chord qualities by ear.

Renaissance period Following the medieval period, the period of musical style between 1450 and 1600.

Requiem Mass A musical setting of the Mass for the dead, named for the opening words of the Introit: *Requiem aeternam dona eis, Domine* ("Rest eternal grant to them, Lord").

resolution The movement from **dissonance** to **consonance** in music (tension to relaxation).

resonance The intensification and enhancement of sound through vibration in the resonating cavities of the head and chest.

rest A silence of specific duration in music, or the symbol used to denote silence.

rhythm A pattern of musical movement through time. Rhythm works within the beat in each bar of music.

romantic period Following the classical period, the period of musical style between 1825 and 1900.

root See **tonic**.

round See **canon**.

S

SATB Abbreviation for soprano, alto, tenor, and bass; a chorus of mixed (male and female) voices.

scale A succession of musical tones arranged in a stepwise order. Scale comes from the Italian word *scala*, or ladder.

schwa An unstressed, neutral vowel notated as [ə].

score The written form of a musical composition.

semiconsonant See **glide**.

semitone See **half step**.

semivowel See **glide**.

sequence The repetition of a musical pattern on a higher or lower pitch.

sextet A composition for, or a group of, six singers or instrumentalists.

shanty See **chantey**.

sharp A symbol ♯ that raises the pitch of a note one-half step. This term is also used to describe a singer or instrumentalist who plays or sings above the true pitch.

sight-read To sing or play a piece of music at first sight without previous preparation or study.

sixteenth note ♪ A note that is one-half the value of an eighth note. Four sixteenth notes equal one quarter note.

sixty-fourth note ♪ A note that is one-half the value of a thirty-second note. It takes sixteen sixty-fourth notes to equal one quarter note.

slur A curved line placed above or below a series of *different* pitches, indicating that the notes should be performed in a legato style. Compare with **tie**.

soft palate The posterior, fleshy roof of the mouth that sits behind the hard palate and is responsible for closing the nasopharynx during swallowing or speaking; also called *velum*.

sol In solfeggio, the fifth degree of a major scale.

solfège, solfeggio French and Italian terms (respectively) for a method of ear training and sight-reading that uses syllables (e.g., *do, re, mi, fa, sol, la, ti*), called *solmization*, to label musical pitches.

solmization The use of syllables (e.g., *do, re, mi, fa, sol, la, ti*) to represent different scale degrees.

solo From the Italian meaning "alone"; a piece or a passage of a piece sung or played by a single performer.

soloist The musician who plays or sings a solo piece or passage in a musical work.

song A vocal composition, usually for one performer with accompaniment, based on a poetic text.

soprano From the Italian, meaning "above"; describes the highest female voice, boy's voice (**treble**), or adult male voice with an exceptional range.

sotto voce From the Italian, meaning "under the voice"; an instruction for the singer or instrumentalist to perform in a quiet, subdued voice.

SSA Abbreviation for soprano 1, soprano 2, and alto; a women's chorus. Often seen as SSAA, dividing the lower parts into alto 1 and alto 2.

staccato Italian for "detached"; a direction for the singer or instrumentalist, indicated by a dot above or below a note, to shorten or detach a note from its successors; the opposite of **legato**.

staff The five lines and four spaces upon which musical notation is written; also called *stave*.

stanza See **verse**.

stave See **staff**.

stem A straight line either up or down from the note head, included on all note values smaller than a whole note.

strophic A song in which all stanzas of the text are sung to the same music; the opposite of **through-composed**. A hymn is *strophic*.

subdominant The fourth scale degree or a triad built upon the fourth scale degree.

submediant The sixth scale degree or a triad built upon the sixth scale degree.

subtonic Meaning "below the tonic"; the seventh scale degree of a **natural minor scale**, lying one whole step below the tonic.

supertonic Meaning "above the tonic"; the second scale degree, or a chord built upon the second scale degree.

suspension An accented nonharmonic tone used to delay the resolution of a chord, most often at a cadence. The suspension is prepared by the same note and resolved by a note one step lower (e.g., c–c–b; the first C in the chord is the preparation, the second C is the suspension, and the B is the resolution).

syncopation A deliberate disturbance of the normal pulse, causing an accent to occur on an unexpected beat.

T

tactus The 15th- and 16th-century term for *beat*.

tempo From the Italian, meaning "time"; the rate of speed at which the music moves.

temporomandibular joints (TMJs) The joints of the jawbone and skull, located in front of the ears on both sides.

tenor The highest nonfalsetto adult male voice.

ternary form A musical work in three sections, in which the third section is a repeat of the first (A–B–A). The middle section contains different material.

tessitura The average pitch level of a musical work or the range of the voice containing the most beautiful, resonant, and easily produced tones.

texture The density of the musical lines in a composition, with or without accompaniment, as they are played or sung together. The primary musical textures are **monophonic**, **homophonic**, and **polyphonic**.

thirty-second note ♪ A note that is one-half the value of a sixteenth note. It takes eight thirty-second notes to equal one quarter note.

through-composed A piece in which the music progresses continually, using different music for each verse or stanza. The opposite of **strophic**.

ti In solfeggio, the seventh degree (leading tone) of a major scale.

tie A curved line placed above or below two notes of the *same* pitch, indicating that the note values of both should be added together. Compare with **slur**.

timbre The tone color or quality of a sound that distinguishes that sound from other instruments.

time signature See **meter signature**.

tonality The organization of pitches around a key center or tonic note. The opposite of **atonality**.

tone A sound of definite, consistent pitch; the quality of a musical sound.

tonic The first step, and tonal center, of a major or minor scale or a chord built on the first scale degree; also referred to as the *root*.

trachea A tube, approximately 4 1/2 inches in length, situated in front of the esophagus and extending from the larynx to the lungs, used to move air in and out of the body for singing or speaking.

transition See **bridge**.

transpose To ability to change the key to another pitch center.

treble A boy's unchanged voice with a range equivalent to an adult soprano. *Treble* also refers to the highest parts in a musical composition.

treble clef Also called the *G clef*, a sign placed at the beginning of the staff to indicate that the second line up on the staff is the note G, above middle C. The treble clef with the subscript 8 indicates that the pitch is heard an octave lower. This form of the clef is found quite often in the tenor part.

tremolo An undesirable vocal vibrato that is either too fast or two slow.

triad A chord formed by arranging three tones, one above the other, in thirds (e.g., a C-Major triad is c–e–g). The most common types of triads are **major, minor, augmented,** and **diminished**.

trill A musical ornament requiring a rapid alteration of two neighboring pitches.

trio A composition for, or a group of, three singers or instrumentalists.

triphthong Three vowel sounds in succession (e.g., the "ee," "eh," and "ee" sounds made in pronouncing the Italian word *miei*).

triple meter Music with three beats per measure. The most common examples are 3/2, 3/4, 3/8, and 9/8.

triplet A group of three notes performed in the time normally allotted to two, indicated by a "3" above or below the notes, and with brackets for note groupings that are not grouped together.

TTBB Abbreviation for tenor 1, tenor 2, baritone, and bass; a men's chorus.

tuning fork A U-shaped metal instrument that produces a fixed tone when struck.

tutti From the Italian, meaning "all"; an instruction for all performers to sing or play at the same time, typically after a solo section.

20th-century music Following the romantic period, the period of musical style between 1900 and 1999.

21st-century music Following 20th-century music, the modern period of musical style beginning in the year 2000.

U

unison An interval of two notes of the same pitch (perfect unison) or the performance by several singers or instrumentalists on the same notes at once.

upbeat The upward movement of the conductor's hand or baton in preparation for the downbeat to follow; often referred to as a *pickup* or *anacrusis*.

V

velum See **soft palate**.

verse A line of poetry within a poem or hymn that is arranged in a metrical fashion; another word for *poetry* or *stanza*.

vibrato An oscillation of pitch that moves above and below the pitch in a wave-like motion. An even *vibrato* is heard at the rate of about 5 to 7 vibrations per second.

virtuoso A performer with extraordinary command of an instrument. A virtuoso passage in a work requires dazzling technical facility.

voice The vocal instrument housed in the human body; a musical line or part.

volume The magnitude of loudness or softness.

vowel modification An adjustment in the pronunciation of a vowel sound to increase resonance throughout the range.

W

whole note ○ A note that has the value of two half notes or four quarter notes. The whole note is the only note without a stem.

whole step An interval made up of two half steps (e.g., c to d on the piano keyboard).

whole-tone scale A six-note scale made up entirely of whole steps (e.g., c–d–e–f-sharp–g-sharp–a-sharp–b-sharp, which is **enharmonic** with C).

Alderson, Richard. *Complete Handbook of Voice Training*. West Nyack, NY: Parker Publishing, 1979.

Andrews, Joyce. *The Oxford Paperback Italian Dictionary*. Oxford, England: Oxford University Press, 1986.

Apel, Willi. *Harvard Dictionary of Music*. 2nd ed. Cambridge, MA: Belknap Press of Harvard University Press, 1972.

Bennett, Roy C. *The Choral Singer's Handbook: How to Become a Good Choral Singer*. New York: Edward B. Marks Music, 1977.

Benward, Bruce, Barbara Garvey Jackson, and Bruce R. Jackson. *Practical Beginning Theory: A Fundamentals Worktext*. 8th ed. Madison, WI: McGraw-Hill College, 2000.

Chorus America. *America's Performing Art: A Study of Choruses, Choral Singers, and Their Impact*. Washington, DC: Chorus America, 2003.

Coffin, Berton, Ralph Errolle, Werner Singer, and Pierre DeLattre. *Phonetic Readings of Songs and Arias, 2nd ed*. Metuchen, NJ: Scarecrow Press, 1982.

Colorni, Evelina. *Singer's Italian: A Manual of Diction and Phonetics*. New York: G. Schirmer, 1970.

Conable, Barbara. *The Structures and Movement of Breathing: A Primer for Choirs and Choruses*. Chicago: GIA Publishing, 2000.

Cox, Richard. G. *The Singer's Manual of German and French Diction*. New York: G. Schirmer, 1970.

De Angelis, Michael, and Nicola A Montani. *The Correct Pronunciation of Latin According to Roman Usage*. Chicago: GIA Publishing, 1973.

Decker, Harold A., and Colleen J. Kirk. *Choral Conducting: Focus on Communication*. Englewood Cliffs, NJ: Prentice Hall, 1988.

Ehmann, Wilhelm, and Frauke Haasemann. *Voice Building for Choirs*. Chapel Hill, NC: Hinshaw Music, 1982.

Garretson, Robert L. *Choral Music: History, Style, and Performance Practice*. Englewood Cliffs, NJ: Prentice Hall, 1993.

Glenn, Carole. *In Quest of Answers: Interviews With American Choral Conductors*. Chapel Hill, NC: Hinshaw Music, 1991.

Grout, Donald Jay. *A History of Western Music*. 3rd ed., shorter. New York: W. W. Norton, 1981.

Haasemann, Frauke, and James M. Jordan. *Group Vocal Technique*. Chapel Hill, NC: Hinshaw Music, 1991.

Haasemann, Frauke, and James M. Jordan. *Group Vocal Technique: The Vocalise Cards*. Chapel Hill, NC: Hinshaw Music, 1992.

Herman, Sally. *Building a Pyramid of Musicianship*. San Diego, CA: Curtis Music Press, 1988.

Jacobs, Arthur. *The New Penguin Dictionary of Music*. Harmondsworth, Middlesex, England: Penguin Books Limited, 1977.

Jeffers, Ron. *Translations and Annotations of Choral Repertoire*. Vol. 1, *Sacred Latin Texts*. Corvallis, OR: Earthsongs, 1988.

Marshall, Madeleine. *The Singer's Manual of English Diction*. New York: G. Schirmer, 1953.

Moriarty, John. *Diction*. Boston: EC Schirmer, 1975.

Mussulman, Joseph A. *Dear People . . . Robert Shaw: A Biography*. Bloomington: Indiana University Press, 1979.

Paton, John Glenn. *German Diction: The Singer's Guide to Pronunciation*. Van Nuys, CA: Alfred Publishing, 1991.

Sasse, H. C., J. Horne, and Charlotte Dixon. *Cassell's Compact German Dictionary*. New York: Dell, 1966.

Schmid, Will. *Something New to Sing About*. Mission Hills, CA: Glencoe, 1989.

Schmidt, Jan. *Basics of Singing*. New York: Schirmer Books, 1984.

Thornton, Tony. "The History of the Mass, Motet, and Madrigal." Master's project. Baton Rouge, LA: Louisiana State University, 1992.

Ulrich, Homer. *A Survey of Choral Music*. New York: Harcourt Brace Jovanovich, 1973.

Uris, Dorothy. *To Sing in English: A Guide to Improved Diction*. New York: Boosey & Hawkes, 1971.

Vennard, William. *Singing: The Mechanism and the Technic*. New York: Carl Fischer, 1967.

Wright, Craig. *Listening to Music*. St. Paul, MN: West Publishing, 1992.

INDEX

A

Accents, 48-49
Accompaniment, 12, 15, 53, 54
Agility, 42
Air passage, 26-27
Alignment. See Body alignment
American Choral Directors Association (ACDA), 158
American Federation of Television and Recording Artists (AFTRA), 161
American Guild of Musical Artists (AGMA), 161, 171
Atlanta Symphony Chorus, 5
Auditions, 9, 51
  acceptance, 58-59
  anxiety about, 51-52
  callbacks, 56
  completion of, 55
  ensemble selection and, 7-8, 10
  entrance into, 54
  last-minute preparation for, 52-53
  performance suggestions, 54-55
  planning for, 9-10
  rejections, 57-58
  results of, 55-59
  skill-building and, 11
  solo pieces for, 12
  written exams and, 55
    See also Learning process; Rehearsals; Vocal technique

B

Baroque music, 179-181
Bel canto technique, 122
Berkshire Choral Festival, 169
Bernac, Pierre, 14
Black, Andrew, 63, 161

Black folders, 63, 161
Body alignment, 19, 20-21
   holding music, 23, 63
   music stand use, 23
   sitting position, 22
   standing position, 21, 22
   See also Breath management; Vocal technique
Breath management, 13, 19, 24
   air passage and, 26-27
   diaphragm activation exercise, 30
   inhalation/exhalation process, 24-27
   inviting breath and, 26, 34
   jaw positioning and, 25-26
   release of tone, 35
   score marking and, 85
   "slow leak" exercise, 28-29
   surprise breath exercise, 30-31
   vibrato and, 34
   yawn space exercise, 28

C

Catching breath. See Surprise breathing
Chanticleer, 6
Chest voice, 18, 39
Children's choruses, 169
Choral festivals, 169
ChoralNet, 6-7, 157, 175
Choral singing, 1
   benefits of, 3
   groups, search for, 6-7
   participation, rationale for, 2
   summer festivals, 169
   tone deafness and, 2
      See also Auditions; Diction; Ensembles; Learning process; Rehearsals
Chorus America, 1, 3, 5, 58, 158
Chromatic scale, 44-45
Church choirs, 5, 171
Classical music, 181-182

Coffin, Berton, 14
Community choruses, 5
Conductors
    choral conducting profession, 173-175
    early preparation of, 174
    graduate education, 175
    rehearsal responsibilities of, 65-66
    undergraduate education, 174-175
Consonant sounds, 76, 77, 78-79
    English diction, 113-114
    French diction, 140-143
    German diction, 131-134
    Italian diction, 125-128
    Latin (Roman) diction, 118-122
        See also Diction; Text
Copyright restrictions, 74
Crescendo technique, 46-48

D

Decrescendo technique, 47
Delattre, Pierre, 14
Diaphragm activation, 30
Diction, 101
    basic principles of, 101-102
    English diction, 111-115
    French diction, 134-143
    German diction, 128-134
    Italian diction, 122-128
    Latin (Roman) diction, 116-122
    singing practice and, 102-103
    song preparation process and, 14
    vowel purity, 35, 36
        See also International Phonetic Alphabet (IPA)
Drop-the-jaw directive, 25-26
Dynamics, 14, 46-48

Educational organizations, 4, 174
English diction, 111
    American R, 115
    consonant sounds, 113-114
    diphthongs, 113
    glides, 113
    neutral vowel sounds, 113
    syllable division, 115
    vowel sounds, 112
Ensembles
    church choirs, 5
    community choruses, 5
    educational organizations and, 4
    nonprofit choral organizations, 5
    professional groups, 6
    search techniques, 6-7
    selection criteria, 7-8, 10
    small group singing, 69-70
    volunteer/professional mix in, 5
        See also Auditions; Choral singing; Rehearsals
Etiquette guidelines, 92-94
Exercises
    accents, 48-49
    agility, 42
    ascending triads, 39-40
    chromatic scale, 44-45
    companion CD for, 20, 50
    crescendo, 46-47
    decrescendo, 47
    diaphragm activation, 30
    energizing tone/pitch, 43-44
    glissando, fifths, 39
    glissando, octaves, 40
    guidelines for, 35-36
    hung-ah, hum/yawn space, 38
    legato, 41, 49
    messa di voce/swell, 47-48
    practice scheduling, 19-20
    range extension, 40-41

repeated pitches, 44
sigh, middle/low range, 37
sigh-pitch connection, 37-38
"slow leak," 28-29
staccato, 41, 49
surprise breath, 30-31
vowel shaping/production, 41-42
whole tone scale, 45-46
yawn space, 28, 38
    See also Body alignment; Breath management; Diction; Vocal technique
Exhalation. See Breath management

F

Festivals, 169
Finale® software, 12
"Fishmouth" shaping, 36
Focused tone, 39
Folders, 63, 161
Foreign language text, 14, 79
   music terminology, 145-149
    See also Diction; International Phonetic Alphabet (IPA)
French diction, 134-135
   consonant sounds, 140-143
   diphthongs/triphthongs, 139-140
   liaison, 143
   nasal vowels, 138, 139
   nonnasal vowels, 135-137, 139
   schwa (e muet), 137-138
   syllable stress, 135
   vowel sounds, 135-140

G

German diction, 128
   consonant sounds, 131-134
   diphthongs, 130
   schwa, 130
   syllable stress, 130
   vowel sounds, 128-130

Glissando technique, 39, 40
Glottal attacks, 33, 36
Groups. See Auditions; Ensembles

H

Haasemann, Frauke, 36
Head voice, 18
Healthy-voice guidelines, 90-92
History. See Music history

I

Inhalation. See Breath management
International Federation of Choral Music (IFCM), 157, 169
International Phonetic Alphabet (IPA), 20, 76, 103
    characters in, 104-105
    chart of, 106-111
    symbols in, 103-104
        See also Diction
Internet resources
    copyright restrictions, 74
    ensembles, search paths for, 6-7
    folders for music, 161
    international choral networks, 157
    national organizations, 158
    private voice study, 11, 158-159
    sheet music suppliers, 160
    theory/sight-reading/history, 159-160
    vocal cords, information on, 33
        See also Software
The Interpretation of French Song, 14
Intonation, 2, 43
    chromatic scale, 44-45
    energizing tone/pitch and, 43-44
    repeated pitches, 44
    score markings and, 79-81
    whole tone scale, 45-46
IPA. See International Phonetic Alphabet (IPA)

Italian diction, 122
   consonant sounds, 125-128
   diphthongs/triphthongs, 124-125
   elision, 124
   glides, 124
   syllable stress, 124
   vowel sounds, 123-124

J

Jaw positioning, 25-26

L

Language. See Diction; Foreign language text; Text
Larynx position, 32
Latin (Roman) diction, 116
   consonant sounds, 118-122
   diphthongs, 117-118
   syllable stress, 117
   vowel sounds, 116-117
Learning process, 13
   accompaniment and, 15
   breath management and, 13
   dynamics and, 14
   memorization techniques, 15
   recordings and, 13, 63, 70, 71
   rhythmic patterns and, 14
   text, focus on, 13-14
     See also Exercises; Practice; Rehearsals; Vocal technique
Leck, Henry, 169
Legato technique, 41, 49
Lift, 18, 19, 36
Listening skills, 2, 46, 66
Los Angeles Opera Chorus, 171

M

Markings. See Score marking
Medieval music, 177
Memorization techniques, 15
Messa di voce technique, 47-48
Middle voice, 18, 39
Modern music, 184-185
Music history, 11, 159
   baroque period, 179-181
   classical period, 181-182
   medieval period, 177
   modern period, 184-185
   Renaissance period, 178-179
   romantic period, 182-183
Musicianship exercises, 43
   accents, 48-49
   chromatic scale, 44-45
   crescendo/decrescendo, 46-47
   energizing tone/pitch, 43-44
   intonation, 43-46
   messa di voce/swell, 47-48
   repeated pitches, 44
   staccato/legato, 49
   whole tone scale, 45-46
     See also Theory; Vocal technique exercises
Musicians' union, 161, 171
Music selections
   auditions and, 12
   learning process and, 13-15
   memorization and, 15
Music terminology, 145
   general terms, 148-149
   music structure terms, 147
   tempo modification terms, 146-147
   tempo range terms, 145-146

N

National Association for Music Education (MENC), 158
National Association of Teachers of Singing (NATS), 11, 159
New-member orientation, 62
Notation software, 12

O

Oregon Bach Festival, 169

P

Pacific Rim Children's Chorus Festival, 169
Performances, 89
    after-concert celebrations, 97-98
    ambassador role and, 90
    audience reaction, 97, 98
    dress rehearsals for, 71-72
    etiquette for, 92-94
    logistics for, 95-97
    preparation for, 94-95
    vocal health, guidelines for, 90-92
        See also Rehearsals; Touring tips
Phrase markings, 85-88
Pitch. See Intonation
Posture. See Body alignment
Practice, 19-20
    body alignment and, 20-21
    guidelines for, 35-36
        See also Diction; Exercises; Rehearsals; Vocal technique
Preparation. See Auditions; Learning process; Rehearsals; Vocal technique
Professional singers, 6, 68, 171
Pronunciation. See Diction; International Phonetic Alphabet (IPA)

R

Range. See Registers; Vocal ranges
Range extension, 40-41

Reading skills. See Sight-reading skills
Recording devices, 13, 63
Recording sessions, 163-164
Registers, 18-19, 36
Rehearsals, 61
    conductors, responsibilities of, 65-66
    dress rehearsals, 71-72
    extra rehearsals, 69-70
    full-scale rehearsals, 64
    guidelines for, 68-69
    initial rehearsal, 62
    materials for, 62-63
    new-member orientations, 62
    private rehearsal and, 70-71
    professional singers and, 68
    recording devices and, 63
    rehearsal CDs and, 70
    short rehearsals, 64
    sight-reading and, 69
    singers, responsibilities of, 66-67
    small group rehearsals, 71
    structure of, 63-64
        See also Performances; Score marking
Renaissance music, 178-179
Resonance chambers, 19
Retreats, 69
Rhythmic patterns, 14, 83-84
Rilling, Helmut, 169
Romantic music, 182-183

S

San Francisco Symphony Chorus, 171
School ensembles, 4, 174
Score marking, 62, 73-74
    general markings, 74-76
    intonation markings, 79-81
    phrase markings, 85-88
    tempo/rhythm markings, 82-84
    tone/text markings, 76-79

Search techniques, 6-7
Shaw, Robert, 5, 14
Sheet music suppliers, 160
Sibelius software, 12
Sigh technique, 27, 32, 33, 34, 37, 41
Sight-reading skills, 11, 69, 80, 155-156
Singer, Werner, 14
Small group singing, 69-70
Soft palate positioning, 25-26, 38
Software
    notation program, 12
        See also Internet resources
Solfège, 45, 80
Solo pieces, 12, 53, 54
        See also Auditions; Learning process
Sore throats, 33
Sound production, 19, 31-32
        See also Body alignment; Breath management; Intonation; Vocal technique
Speaking-in-rhythm, 14
Staccato technique, 41, 49
Summer choral festivals, 169
Surprise breathing, 30-31
Swell technique, 47-48

T

Teachers
    audition preparations and, 11-12
    text translation and, 14
        See also Internet resources; Learning process
Tempo markings, 82-83, 145-147
Terminology. See Music terminology
Text, 13-14
    score markings, 76-79
    speaking-in-rhythm, 14
    translations of, 14, 79
        See also Diction; International Phonetic Alphabet (IPA)

Theory, 11, 14
   audition requirements and, 55
   Internet resources, 159-160
   key signatures, 151-152
   music terminology, 145-149
      See also Musicianship exercises; Score marking; Sight-reading skills
Throat soreness, 33
Tone deafness, 2
Touring tips, 165-167
Translations, 14, 79

U

Union membership, 161, 171

V

Vibrato, 34
Visualization, 12, 15, 34
Vocal cords, 33, 36
Vocal ranges, 154
   classification system, 153
   range extension exercises, 40-41
   registers, 18-19, 36
Vocal technique, 17-18, 34-35
   auditions and, 11, 12
   open-jaw positioning and, 25-26
   practice, role of, 19-20
   registers, 18-19, 36
   sound production, 19, 31-32
   vibrato, 34
   vocal cords and, 33
   warm-up process, 13, 20
      See also Body alignment; Breath management; Exercises; Learning process;
         Vocal technique exercises
Vocal technique exercises, 35
   agility, 42
   ascending triads, 39-40
   glissando, fifths, 39

glissando, octaves, 40
guidelines for, 35-36
hung-ah, hum/yawn space, 38
legato-staccato, 41
range extension, 40-41
sigh, middle/low range, 37
sigh-pitch connection, 37-38
vowel shaping/production, 41-42
    See also Musicianship exercises
Volunteer community choruses, 5
Vowel shaping, 36, 39, 41-42
  English diction, 112-113
  French diction, 135-140
  German diction, 128-130
  Italian diction, 123-124
  Latin (Roman) diction, 116-117
    See also Diction; Text

W

Warm-up process, 13, 20
Westminster Choir College of Rider University, 4, 169
Whole tone scale, 45-46
Word-by-Word Translations of Songs and Arias, 14
World Youth Choir/World Children's Choir, 169

Y

Yawn space, 25-26, 28, 32, 34, 38